Musical Guide to In The Court Of The Crimson King by King Crimson

by Andrew Keeling

Edited by Mark Graham
A Spaceward Publication

Copyright ©
2009 Andrew Keeling, Mark Graham and Robert Fripp

Published by Spaceward, Cambridge, UK

ISBN9780956297709

FIRST EDITION - viii, MMIX

blurb

blurb.com

Table of Contents

Photograph of King Crimson	4
Preface	5
Acknowledgements	7
Introduction	9
Photograph of King Crimson Mk.1	12

Part 1

1. King Crimson Mk 1	13
2. Giles, Giles and Fripp	17
3. The Brondesbury Tapes	21
4. Ian McDonald & Peter Sinfield	25
5. Musical Influences	29
6. Music of the Period	37
7. The Counter-culture and Zeitgeist of the 1960's	45
8. Protest and Strategy	53
9. Progressive Rock	57
10. Fantasy and the world of Peter Sinfield	61

Part 2

11. The Minutiae of In the Court of the Crimson King	71
12. The Sound World of In the Court of the Crimson King	111
13. Coda - Contextualising In the Court of the Crimson King	123
Bibliographical Notes	127
Bibliography	131
Links	133
Photographs	135
About The Author	147

Please note that musical examples and diagrams referred to in the text fall at the end of each chapter.

Musical Guide to In The Court Of The Crimson King by King Crimson

King Crimson

Preface

As the world enters yet another period of crisis, this time with potential global financial meltdown compounded by the culture of political-correctness killing the personal liberties of the individual, together with the ever-present threat of terrorism and ongoing problems in the Middle East, King Crimson's epic first album, In the Court of the Crimson King, is as relevant now as it was in 1969 when first released. A recent TV programme documenting the Progressive Rock movement had author Paul Stump saying that ITCOTCK (as I shall refer to it) was the initial statement of the Progressive rock movement. Initially an observation of the period in which it was written, in particular the Vietnam war, ITCOTCK has continued in relevance to each subsequent decade since its release, none more so than now some forty years later. I first heard the album on December 11th, 1969, after a school carol service. The effect it had on me, as a listener and young person, was decisive. I can honestly say that, personally speaking, no other music has struck me in quite the same way. It was the completeness - which today I'd call wholeness - of the music that impacted upon my young psyche; the musicianship and cover-art, composition and poetry had an effect so profound that I decided there and then to explore exactly what it was that was happening within it. I wrote to guitarist Robert Fripp and mellotron/reeds-man Ian McDonald quite soon after. Robert replied more or less immediately; Ian in 2001 quoting the letter over the phone which I'd written him thirty two years previously. Gradually, I began to unravel what was there only to find that the members of the band to whom I spoke were as surprised by it all as I'd been. At times they'd struggle to verbalise the uncanny events, as well as the remarkable reception, surrounding their meteoric rise and, particularly, ITCOTCK. The spirit of the age - the *zeitgeist* - was in some way responsible. 'You had to be there' as people say. However, it was as though there was something greater in King Crimson than mere personalities, music, poetry and art. Gustav Mahler once said that 'One does not compose; one is composed.' Having thought about it long and hard, and having tried to wriggle my way out of this quest as best I can, I think that's probably true in the case of King Crimson. Without wanting to sound completely daft I can say that this music changed my life in more ways than one. I also have to confess to not being a writer. I write music not words, so I apologise if what is written here is in any way misinformed. There is always the tendency to project whatever lies within us onto the outer world. It happens with writers. It has to as a container for enthusiasms, which is the reason for this document. Also, one can analyse music but can't necessarily say how it's played. It's impossible to document pick on string, finger on key, lip on reed or word in throat. And, putting my many misgivings about musical analysis aside, I hope the reader will find something here of value. If it all gets too much then please go back to the music because it's that that counts, after all.

The main concern of this analysis is to show the musical coherence, none more so than in the melodic and harmonic contexts. It's my experience that jazz, rock and folk musicians often work unconsciously, to a large degree. By this I mean they tend to take an instrument and find what sounds good on it for them personally. Sound being their main interest, they are less inclined to write down the result. This way of working has been referred to as the aural tradition. The way fingers fall on keys, or fingers on fret is often the beginning of the creative process and is, of course, different in every case, most often differentiated by technical skill(s), vocal ability and musical influences. Analysis can, if used properly, reveal a further level of musical appreciation.

Acknowledgements

I would like to thank Robert Fripp for his friendship, countless E-mails and letters, and corrections to my assumptions, as well as for permission to reproduce musical examples and other material. Equal thanks goes to Ian McDonald, Peter Sinfield, Michael Giles and Greg Lake who talked to me, sometimes at great length and expense to themselves, about the first King Crimson. Gratitude to Peter Giles for permission to include material from The Cheerful Insanity of Giles, Giles and Fripp. Thank you, Iain Cameron, for your personal perspective on the 1960's. I am indebted to Mark Graham who spent countless hours on the design and layout for this publication. Without your commitment this would never have happened. I am grateful to Jason Walsh for helping me out when time was in short supply, and to Sid Smith for the exhaustive and definitive account of King Crimson in his book, In the Court of King Crimson. To Kevin Price: thank you for being 'ears' to my ideas about King Crimson on countless Lake District walks, and thanks for your ideas too. Hugh O'Donnell, thank you for the photos of King Crimson Mk I. For this analysis I have used King Crimson, In The Court Of The Crimson King CD - Original Master Edition, 2004 (DGM0501). (Andrew Keeling - March, 2009)

Introduction

While some studies on rock music tend to concentrate on political statements, my own approach will be mainly musical. I will, however, include sections on the background to the period as King Crimson's meteoric rise to fame is down to certain key factors which I aim to overview so as to reach an understanding of the band and, ultimately, the success of In the Court of the Crimson King.

First, during Part 1 of the Musical Guide, I will include an overview of the Mk I version of the band, Giles, Giles and Fripp I and II – the band which preceded KC Mk I – Ian McDonald and Peter Sinfield, as well as a section dealing with some of their possible musical influences.

Secondly, the counter-culture of the 1960's was mirrored by King Crimson who, in this context, appeared at exactly the right time and in the right place to encapsulate some of the period's collective aims. With this end in view I will briefly discuss the ethos of the counter-culture and the *zeitgeist* of the 1960's.

Thirdly, the band had a well-defined strategy: not so much a business plan as a plan of action. This coincides with their early style which may be regarded, in part, as a logical extension of the Protest song genre of the early to mid 1960's. King Crimson transcend this by assimilating styles from a number of sources to eventually define the genre Progressive rock, although they never subscribed to the term.

Mainly, although not exclusively, through the band's lyricist Peter Sinfield, they developed a fantasy-like narrative to project their message to a waiting audience. With reference to this I will discuss 'fantasy' prompted, in part, by a reading of Allan F. Moore's Rock the Primary Text (1). This will include a brief analysis of the lyrics of ITCOTCK.

Part 2 of the Musical Guide will concentrate on musical analyses of the songs themselves.

Musical Guide to In The Court Of The Crimson King by King Crimson

King Crimson Mk 1

Part 1.
1. King Crimson Mk I

King Crimson's rise from local obscurity to international success is one of the better known histories of recent rock music history. (2) The band grew out of the Decca-signed trio Giles, Giles and Fripp who made one album, The Cheerful Insanity of Giles, Giles and Fripp, in 1968 along with two 45-rpm singles, One in a Million and Thursday Morning. This Bournemouth trio - Peter Giles, his brother Michael and Robert Fripp - whose musical experiences had included work in hotel bands, dance bands and pop combos (3) - were joined by ex-armed forces bandsman Ian McDonald on June 7th, 1968, along with ex-Fairport Convention vocalist, Judy Dyble. Although this second version of Giles, Giles and Fripp can now be regarded as the prototype version of King Crimson, it would have to wait until the departure of Peter Giles and Judy Dyble in favour of Poole-based vocalist and guitarist Greg Lake, formerly of The Gods, to be brought in as vocalist/bassist on December 2nd of the same year for the official start of the new band. (4)

The band began rehearsals in the basement of the Fulham Palace Cafe on January 13th, 1969, including in their repertoire such songs as The Beatles' Lucy in the Sky with Diamonds and Joni

Mitchell's Michael from the Mountains. Other songs included Fripp's Drop In and Lake's Lucky Man. During these rehearsals Peter Sinfield, McDonald's co-writer, began the construction of a light show for the band. From February 23rd to March 1st, with Peter Sinfield working as roadie, the band embarked on their first residency at a Newcastle-upon-Tyne night-club. It was here that the name King Crimson, coined by Sinfield, was first adopted giving the band its strong, almost diabolic persona, although Michael Giles never formally agreed to it. Subsequently the band began to make its presence felt on the London scene with an early gig at the Speakeasy Club on April 9th. It was then decided that Sinfield should be brought into the group as a fully-fledged member, as lyricist, designer, sound and lighting engineer.

The band continued with celebrated gigs at venues such as the Revolution on May 14th watched by Jimi Hendrix. Musicians like Steve Hackett (guitarist with Genesis) and Bill Bruford (then of Yes and later with King Crimson) saw the band at these early concerts. The historic appearance with the Rolling Stones in Hyde Park, commemorating the death of Brian Jones, took place on July 5th. (5) Following a fated recording with Moody Blues' producer Tony Clarke at Morgan Studios, the band entered Wessex Studios, with themselves producing, to record ITCOTCK. The album was completed on August 20th and released on October 10th, 1969. Mark Williams, reporting in the International Times, called it 'the ultimate album.' Rolling Stone's Jonathan Green called it 'incredibly pretentious' having a 'lack of positive force.' On October 29th the band performed their first US gig in Boston, and later in the tour at the Kinetic Playground in Chicago their equipment was destroyed in an arson attack by the Mob for non-payment of 'insurance'. On December 5th, the LA Times commented about their concert at Hollywood's Whiskey A Go: 'King Crimson are known as a Progressive rock group...dealing in poetic, image-laden lyrics... and play (songs) nothing less than 10 minutes (in length).' Whilst driving from Los Angeles to Big Sur on December 7th, Ian McDonald told Robert Fripp that he and Michael Giles had decided to leave the band. Fripp wrote: 'My stomach disappeared. King Crimson was everything to me. To keep the band together I offered to leave instead, but Ian said that the band was more me than them.' (6) Greg Lake subsequently left to form a new group with Keith Emerson from The Nice and Carl Palmer of Atomic Rooster which became Emerson, Lake and Palmer.

In 1969, unlike the 1980's and beyond, light entertainment was the route by which young musicians negotiated success. From 1965 onwards talented musicians generally served an apprenticeship through pubs, working-mens clubs, hotels and cabaret. Entrepreneurs seized on the potential of young performers by booking them to appear in theatres and in variety shows. Ultimately, this led to appearances on national TV. Broadly speaking, this was the route taken by the members of King Crimson I. At the time work was available for musicians of all kinds, and from the middle of the 1960's the rock club had grown up operating alongside its older parent the blues and jazz club, and complimented by the more intimate setting of the folk club and coffee house which, all in all, provided diverse musical forms for an equally diverse audience. Jazz, blues, pop and folk musicians mingled along with some classical musicians who possessed formal training, to include a wide diversity of musics within their individual and gradually collective repertoires. The 1960's was a time of liberation, not just politically, but also culturally by fuelling diversity. It is from this unique melting-pot of musical styles that King Crimson was born: Robert Fripp as guitar teacher, with experience in hotel jazz bands and rock n'roll bands; Greg Lake from rock/pop bands; Michael Giles from rock and roll bands and Trendsetters Ltd; Ian McDonald from the army school of music, Kneller Hall, and UK forces bands; Peter Sinfield as folk musician, poet and lyricist. This diversity is difficult to grasp today, as from the 1980's onwards there were fewer hotels and clubs offering 'live' entertainment. Also, cabaret and variety theatres had almost vanished. TV is now the place where artists are manufactured and are not, in the main, grounded in 'live' performance. Ex-Nick Drake sidesman Iain Cameron also thinks that location is an important factor for the way in which music was disseminated in the London of the 1960s. 'Basically you have to understand the geography of London. The key road is the South Circular. Musicians in their teens living within three miles of that road are likely to have heard radical electric blues during the period 1964-66, which had an incredible impact in connecting with jazz at a later date. The road connects Ealing, Richmond, Wimbledon, Dulwich and Goldsmiths which all had important venues.' (7)

2. Giles, Giles and Fripp

The Cheerful Insanity of Giles, Giles and Fripp (Deram, 1968) is an aptly named album covering most musical styles available to the period, alongside a surreal kind of humour. TCI (as I shall refer to it) has a similar concept of observation that is realised more fully in the counter-cultural terms of the late 1960's/early '70's.

As I have already suggested, location, background and experience have a distinct bearing on the contribution a musician makes to his/her culture. Musicians, often unable to emulate their close contemporaries, rely on musical weaknesses by making a strength of them. Giles, Giles and Fripp coming from outside of London were, no doubt, aware of the emerging fashions from the capital, but may have felt unable to fully take on these influences or, perhaps, decided not to. Certainly, the trio demonstrate little in the way of blues influence, but jazz features prominently on the album. Robert Fripp's guitar style is confined to Wes Montgomery, Tal Farlow and classical styles treated in a non-fingerstyle, plectrum technique and jazz styles (the chords of Digging My Lawn, the octaves in North Meadow and the clean timbre which would come fully to fruition on In the Wake of

Poseidon and Lizard). The Crukster does however, include dissonant chords and unmetred passages anticipating the later Groon (the B-side of King Crimson's single Catfood [1970]): See Example 1.

Peter Giles' bass playing uses octave displacement in Newly Weds reminiscent of the bass riff found on the King Crimson single Catfood (1970): See Example 2.

The bass riffs are often jazz-like although there is some reference to Paul McCartney's style, while his 'observational' lyrics deal with pastoral (North Meadow) and subjective types (Newly Weds). Michael Giles' inventive drumming shows the influence of Elvin Jones and Tony Williams, William Blake-like poetry (The Crukster) and surreal, Bonzo Dog Doo-Dah Band-style humour (Just George). The Giles brothers' playing and harmony vocals point forward to some of the music found on McDonald and Giles (Island, 1970), the album made by McDonald and Giles after leaving King Crimson.

Some textural variety is found on TCI, alongside the vocals, guitar, bass and drums line-up. For example, mellotron is featured on One in a Million and Little Children. Chamber strings appear on Thursday Morning, the beginning of which is highly reminiscent of The Beatles' Strawberry Fields Forever: See Example 3. Piano, organ and voice alone are heard on Call Tomorrow. Fripp's spoken monologue, The Saga of Rodney Toady, is used as a connective device throughout the first side of the album relating the story of a young misfit and his parents. (8) This is part and parcel of the observation to which I referred previously, which also include early marriage (Newly Weds), love and unwanted pregnancy (Call Tomorrow) and, realisation and suffering (The Crukster).

In purely musical terms TCI has a wide variety of sources. Harmonically speaking, Thursday Morning is Beatles inspired: See Example 4.

Little Children references 1960's big band and light pop, but the guitar chords fall off the beat, not to mention dyads that are culled from the chords themselves. Satire is at the back of the album especially on One in a Million and The Elephant Song. Call Tomorrow utilises a Procul Harum-like descending bass line in a chorale or hymn-like style with its quasi-religious subject about a vicar's daughter: See Example 5.

Digging My Lawn is an example of cool jazz, the introduction comprising added-note chords: Dmaj11, G13, C maj7 (Cmaj9), A (7)13. In The Crukster, Bartok-like lines approach free-form jazz styles, although the guitar line is metreless and used as an accompaniment for Michael Giles' spoken poetry. Music Hall is the basis for The Sun is Shining while Suite No.1 eventually becomes a Jacques Lousier influenced classical-jazz arrangement. The A-B-C multi-sectional form of this piece points forward to some Progressive rock styles. Erudite Eyes is the most forward-looking piece by including improvisation over a drone. The guitar parts anticipate some of Fripp's sustained guitar lines on In the Wake of Poseidon which is, existentially, the reconvening of Giles, Giles and Fripp under the name of King Crimson.

It goes without saying that the wide stylistic variety of TCI had a bearing on King Crimson. Essentially, it is two fifths of the membership of King Crimson. I suggest that it is a prototype ITCOTCK without the extrovert power of Greg Lake or the multi-instrumental strengths of Ian McDonald. Nor does it have the countercultural interests of Peter Sinfield who added a vital twist to the emerging group. Michael Giles has said: 'TCI came about because of our humour and the satirists who were around at the time: Spike Milligan, Peter Cooke and Dudley Moore and so on. We also knew Frank Zappa's early records and had worked with members of the Bonzo Dog Doo-Dah Band. At the time the three of us were trying to get upstate and into the future. Erudite Eyes is a halfway stage as it represents the way we were wanting to do things which were original and break out and play out and we nearly got there. Peter and Robert didn't agree on the way forward. We wanted to break out and be released from the frustrations of living in a place like Bournemouth where, unlike Liverpool or London or any big city, there's no social unrest although there was a thriving scene, given the endless list of musicians who've come from there.' (9) Robert Fripp has elaborated on the position: 'In GG&F the basic cotton wool jazz guitar sound was enough...I wanted a Marshall stack and a Les Paul cranked-up.' (10)

Ex. 1

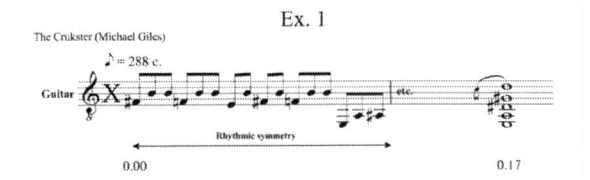

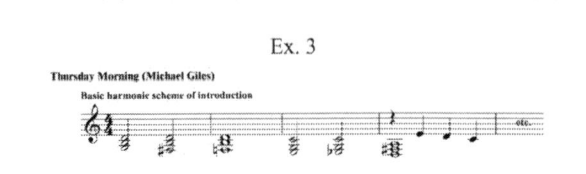

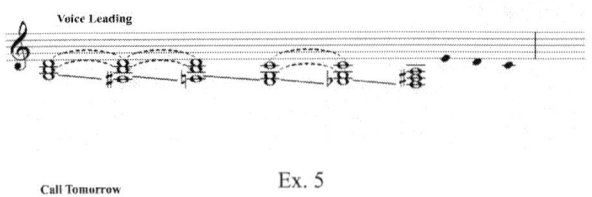

The Crukster (Michael Giles) — Guitar
Rhythmic symmetry
0.00 — 0.17

Ex. 2

Newly Weds (Peter Giles) — Bass Guitar
0.00 — 0.02

Ex. 3

Thursday Morning (Michael Giles)
Basic harmonic scheme of introduction

Ex. 4

Voice Leading

Ex. 5

Cali Tomorrow — Organ / Piano
0.00 — 0.30

3. The Brondesbury Tapes - Giles, Giles and Fripp II

This album, released by Aluna Records in 2001 (VP235CD), is historically important in the development of King Crimson, because of the input of Ian McDonald both at an instrumental and writing level. His presence was also significant in introducing Peter Sinfield as a writer and conceptualist.

McDonald had briefly played alongside Sinfield in the latter's band, Creation. It was following a performance of the original version of The Court of the Crimson King that McDonald turned to Sinfield uttering the immortal words: 'Look Peter, someone has to tell you. Your band is absolutely hopeless...still, you write some interesting words. Why don't we write a couple of songs together?' (11) TBT (as I shall refer to it) includes some prototype versions of music from ITCOTCK alongside music featured on TCI recorded at 93A, Brondesbury Road, London, NW6, where Giles, Giles and Fripp lived and rehearsed during their time in London. Peter Giles recorded the songs on a Revox F36 two-track tape recorder. The personnel on the songs is represented by Giles, Giles and Fripp sometimes augmented by McDonald and sometimes including ex-Fairport Convention, then soon-to-be Trader Horne vocalist, Judy Dyble.

Besides I Talk to the Wind which appears twice (once with Judy Dyble and once without her), Erudite Eyes (from TCI) appears augmented by McDonald's flute playing; (Why don't you just) Drop In (a Fripp composition re-written with new words by Sinfield and appearing on the 1971 King Crimson album, Islands as The Letters, as well as being a stable part of King Crimson Mk I repertoire known as Drop In); Under the Sky, a McDonald-Sinfield composition (although here credited to Fripp) which appeared on Sinfield's 1973 album, Still; Make It Today, another McDonald-Sinfield song, is of particular interest as it fits like a glove into Giles, Giles and Fripp's repertoire in a post-Fairport Convention I style. ...Drop In is the first piece to signal something of a stylistic change with the more strident opening, the verse riff and tight three-part harmony vocals which anticipate the later vocal arrangements heard on McDonald and Giles (1970). It also includes a guitar solo (1:25) which augurs the shape of things to come in terms of some of Fripp's later playing. Jazz stylisms remain the central diet of the band, particularly with the Fripp filler solo at 0:55 of ...Drop In, although the rest of this song is close to some contemporary rock of the period. The first version of I Talk to the Wind, represented here, is structured similarly to the version found on ITCOTCK, although it is in A Major and rhythmically more foursquare. Featuring McDonald on acoustic guitar and on flute (double-tracked) it includes an electric guitar solo by Fripp, dialoguing with McDonald's flute from 2:10. Three-part harmony vocals are also featured in the final verse. These songs, including Under the Sky, point to the future. The satirical humour found on TCI is eclipsed by a greater sense of gravitas, and the gorgeousness of McDonald's melodic and harmonic gift begins to make its presence felt in the hands of able players. This had the tendency to develop Fripp's writing if Plastic Pennies and Passages of Time are anything to go by, illustrating his interest in multi-sectional forms with sections of contrasting music. Passages of Time is heard as a prototype of the ascending section of Bolero from Lizard two years later, and the final Peace from In the Wake of Poseidon in 1970 (Passages of Time - 1:42). One has the feeling that after the departure of McDonald and Giles from King Crimson in December 1969, Fripp and Sinfield were forced into utilising some of this earlier material to produce In the Wake of Poseidon and, further, Lizard and Islands. Passages of Time is characterised by a harmonic shift not unlike that found in some Spanish guitar music: See Example 6.

It is also possible to detect the musical differences that were arising between Peter Giles and the remaining members. Paradoxically, whilst Peter Giles was distanced from the gradually emerging style of the other members, it was Ian McDonald and Michael Giles who were to return to the mercurial sensitivity of his style which can be heard on their eponymous album of 1970, on which he played as a session musician. However, the coda of Murder, from 2:19, certainly points towards some of the free-form improvisatory moments of King Crimson Mk I. The instrumental section of Erudite Eyes, from 1:30ff, anticipates one or two of the 'live' improvisations heard on King Crimson's Epitaph (DGM 9607, 1997), and on Get Thy Bearings, Mantra and Travel Weary Capricorn to be found on the recent Hyde Park Club release. I believe it was at this moment (i.e. the coda of Erudite Eyes) that, musically speaking, King Crimson was born and where the jazz-like workouts of the band has its beginnings. It required Greg Lake's vocal power and his more direct approach to bass playing in a rock context, to make the transition from 1960's whimsical satirists to the coherent and cohesive counter-cultural unit. At the same time I also suggest that the humorous side of King Crimson had its beginnings in Peter Giles' approach, which was subsequently transformed by the more fashionable counter-cultural vision of Peter Sinfield. It was as though King Crimson began to court musical risks possibly borne from musical frustration. Fripp has noted: 'The energy of frustration fuelled our efforts. We all had lame professional experiences which pointed ways not to go in music. So, we resolved to play what we wished to play...and figured if we were good enough we might earn a living.' (12) In taking these risks the band took the step of entering the wider counter-cultural scene and crossed stylistic boundaries with music that covered rock, jazz, folk and classical styles. In this way they became an important connection with middle-class sensibilities so important to the counter-culture, as suddenly the whole became greater than the sum of the parts.

Ex. 6

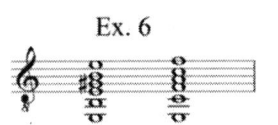

4. Ian McDonald and Peter Sinfield

Ian McDonald had been trained as a clarinettist at Kneller Hall, the army music school, where he also received formal lessons in harmony, orchestration and aural. He was self-taught on sax and flute. After leaving the army and returning to the UK, he spotted an advert for 'musicians wanted' in the Melody Maker and, together with flautist and guitarist Iain Cameron, applied and got the gig. The band was called Tintagel.

Iain Cameron has said: 'Tintagel was a student acid rock band based in Goldsmiths College Drama Department. Ian lived near me and had a minivan and so he would drive me round the South Circular beyond Greenwich to rehearse. Our repertoire was a lot of Love (from Da Capo), some Byrds, some Doors, some originals. A week after we joined we both did a Tintagel gig at the Middle Earth in Covent Garden. Fairport Convention, with Judy Dyble, were on the bill. We got to see lots of underground stars - The Nice, Principal Edwards, Brian Augur, Arthur Brown etc. Tintagel's instrumentation was bass, drums, someone who doubled Danelectro 12-string guitar and sitar plus Ian and myself. I think the sitar/flute/12-string sound was quite good for its time, and Ian tried to kick the band into a more professional shape, possibly due to his training. He was sensibly looking for a band that was going to go places which Tintagel was almost, but not quite. But Ian had worked it out within a couple of months that he wanted to go higher and faster. He had met Judy Dyble at that first gig, and when Sandy Denny took over the Fairports he started a band with Judy. This kind of merged with Giles, Giles and Fripp. The rest is history.' (13) (Iain Cameron went on to Cambridge University where he met Nick Drake, and played flute for him on several occasions).

Peter Sinfield had a very Bohemian upbringing. (14) From age 8 to 13, he was sent to school in the country, and from 13 to 14 was at the City of London School living with his mother in Kensington. From 14 to 16 he was back in the country at Bracknell New Town and from 17 to 27 lived in London. After he left school he 'went into computers, hung around with friends from Chelsea Arts School and started to write bits of poetry. I bought a copy of Bert Weedon's Play in a Day guitar book - it's true, it teaches you how to play a song called Sinner Man in A Minor and E Minor. I got lucky and met a guy called Ian McDonald.' (15) After playing together in Sinfield's band, Creation, they began writing and Sinfield re-wrote In the Court of the Crimson King. Sinfield remembers that the song 'originally had two chords - E Minor and A Minor - with the first lines: "Shadows from a falling sun lie black across my road." We also wrote two other pop songs in a Procul Harum vein, "Springtime Song" and "Another Day".' (16) Sinfield had relatives who belonged to 'The Men of Trees', 'a group saturated in esoterica and on the fringes of Notting Hill bohemian circles which quite probably included members of The Golden Dawn...I was somewhat exposed to the occult.' (17)

Sinfield's role in King Crimson was similar to Keith Reid's in Procul Harum as lyricist and non-performing member, except that Sinfield was responsible for the initial concept of King Crimson, the name and the 'essence' of the band. Robert Fripp has suggested that McDonald and Sinfield 'helped free up the thinking space' (18) by providing the emerging band with an approach to counter-cultural thinking and the *zeitgeist*. McDonald had seen many of the new bands on the underground scene, and been trained in classical and jazz styles, which connected with Fripp's and the Giles' interests. Sinfield's poetic and literary sources were invaluable to the developing musical vocabulary and his words began to fit into the scene alongside the imagery of Marc Bolan and Jim Morrison. McDonald's and Sinfield's songwriting is polystylistic. For example, I Talk to the Wind and Under the Sky illustrate folk styles via Fairport Convention, but with the kind of harmonic shifts found in The Beatles via jazz. Certainly, McDonald's style seems more concerned with longer harmonic rhythms than those found in some of the Giles, Giles and Fripp repertoire. The fusion of these styles was to have a direct bearing on the Progressive genre that Fripp has said 'King Crimson helped define.' (19) One wonders, with the inclusion of Judy Dyble at this time, whether Giles, Giles and Fripp II had their sights set on folk rock rather than the final sonic result of King Crimson. Sinfield's input into the visual and conceptual side cannot be underestimated. Because of his mother's unconventional lifestyle he was looked after, at an early age, by a German housekeeper called Maria Wandella, who was a circus highwire walker. In this way the world of entertainment was thrust upon him at an early age. He had turned to literature at Danes Hill Prep School through his English teacher, John Mawson (20). Eventually he turned to the writings of Mervyn Peake, Rimbaud, Alan Watts and the International Times, Oz and other contemporary counter-cultural sources: 'Exploring with the use of substances various, Casteneda, The Tibetan Book of the Dead, The Doors of Perception etc.' Sinfield also thought of the name, King Crimson: 'Granted, the name was taken from The Court of the Crimson King in a moment of great panic. Not the least because it had the brazen impact of Led Zeppelin!' (21) The Crimson King is also the name of a Japanese tree.

By drawing in McDonald and Sinfield it was possible to include a cutting-edge rock, folk, jazz and classical fusion besides a songwriting team of visionary calibre. It only remained for Greg Lake's presence to provide the band with one of the most original and defining voices of the 1970's as well as an assured focal point.

5. Musical Influences

Often, a composer only recomposes what he/she has already heard. Sometimes music directly accesses previous works and, at other times, there is a very distant relationship between two works. More often, musicians simply have likes and dislikes which tend not to feed into their own works. The musical and extra-musical influences of the first King Crimson are many and diverse, and I have discussed these with the five members mainly because I am interested to discover if what they listened to had any bearing on ITCOTCK in terms of its music and its structural properties. I am also interested in preceding the subsequent section, on the counter-culture and the *zeitgeist*, with key albums of the period to give readers some indication of the cultural properties of the time in terms of its music. I do not believe that ITCOTCK fell from the sky, as it were, but nor do I believe that influences were simply copied. All great art comes into being mysteriously, and great music bears the hallmarks of influences that have been transformed in the hands of masters.

Robert Fripp

AK: I am guessing your influences re guitar on the Giles, Giles and Fripp period were Tal Farlow, Wes Montgomery and the classical guitar work of John Williams, though in a plectrum style.

RF: Not particularly any of these, although not-not either. The Moto Perpetuo on Suite in A (on TCI) was more in response to Paganini's although very, very much feebler! The brief overview is this: the influences were not so much individual players as much as pieces of music, or approaches to music; mainly as part of my learning to play the guitar. So, the classical side was drawn from classical guitar pieces, and an interest in violin pieces. The jazzier side from learning chord substitution and working in Bournemouth hotels. The rockier side from early rock artists. And, alongside this, listening on records and live performance. BMG was a magazine for fretted instruments that I began taking around 13, and it had a 4-page music supplement every month for banjo, plectrum and classical guitar, mandolin. I worked through a lot of these. Also Carcassi Etudes, Recuerdos de la Alhambra (Tarrega), September in the Rain, Misty, Nola, Orange Blossom Special, Can't Buy Me Love, She Loves You...a broad repertoire! My aim was to be good enough to play with better players. This meant being able to play pretty well anything I was asked to play. The emphasis was on guitar playing at the time, rather than composition or songwriting.

AK: The Brondesbury Tapes, last take of Erudite Eyes (track 17) with Ian McDonald on flute, sounds to me like the moment that King Crimson was born, musically speaking.

RF: It was clear to me that Giles, Giles and Fripp were very good players but had nothing to play. The brothers' writing was songwriting, not players' music. So, Erudite Eyes was an early attempt to get a springboard to improvisation. I did the same with the players at the Majestic Hotel in Bournemouth. They were exceptionally good jazzmen who hadn't clicked that you could improvise over rock music.

AK: How much of an influence was the Moody Blues' Days of Future Passed on King Crimson in terms of its structural concept. I ask because Dawn is a Feeling has a very similar vocal delivery to Greg Lake's and there is something about the harmony too.

RF: Not much really. It showed that you could make a mellotron do some work! Nights in White Satin was magic. But they weren't players. (22)

Ian McDonald

AK: Who were your main influences?

IM: Neil Young, Stravinsky, John Handy, Richard Strauss, Miles Davies, Iron Butterfly... (23) I picked up on whatever was around. The Fairports influenced me especially. Maybe I was subconsciously hoping to put a new Fairports-type band together when I joined Giles, Giles and Fripp. Make It Today on The Brondesbury Tapes is particularly close to early Fairports. The chromatic bit from ITCOTCK which leads back into the mellotron refrain was influenced by Sam and Dave, and the flute turns at the end of the solo on the same track was directly influenced by Rimsky-Korsakov's Scheherazade. I like a lot of Russian classical music particularly. It has a warmth that the avant-garde lacked. 'Feel', for me, is very important. Neil Young I like because he also knows what he wants even before it's been recorded. Neil Young thinks big! I had a couple of Moody Blues albums but was less impressed when they began to use all that narrative. Peter Sinfield likes Nights in White Satin. It was their use of the mellotron which I brought into King Crimson. Graham Bond was OK. Cream were good. I loved the original Yardbirds and the early Pink Floyd, too. The Beatles were also a huge influence. (24)

Peter Sinfield

AK: Can you cite your main influences?

PS: Sonny Rollins, Mahler, J.S. Bach, Poulenc Organ Concerto, Satie and Debussy, lots of world music - especially Chinese and Japanese and gamelan - John Fahey. (25) I wanted King Crimson to move towards the soundworld of Weather Report or Miles Davis' Bitches Brew after Islands. Robert wanted to get away from the soundworld of Lizard. (26) I saw Pink Floyd once at the Commonwealth Institute with Dik Fraser in c.1968. And I took notice of their primitive lightshow! (27) Casteneda, the Tibetan Book of the Dead and The Doors of Perception were all influential. And IT, OZ, Rimbaud, Ram Dass. (28) Edith Sitwell's A Poet's Notebook. (29) Bob Dylan, Donovan, Nick Drake. I liked the influential Forever Changes by Love and Five Leaves Left by Nick Drake both of which I play every full moon. (30) Basho, Dylan Thomas, Gibran, Shakespeare. (31) Even more important was Fairy Tale by Donovan. When I heard and saw him sing 'Yellow is the colour of my true love's hair in the morning...' I remember thinking, 'I could do that!' Influence perhaps to be seen in Moonchild? (32) I was a real fan of Tod Dockstader (real Musique Concrete...or what he called 'organised sound') He made/wrote...a fascinating piece based upon the re-recording of sellotape being pulled up from balloons...sped up, slowed down and layered. I think this was in 1964. He also recorded an album called Quatermass. When one evening I heard the mainframe computer (a Leo 3) which I was employed to run, happily bleep the tone of Daisy, Daisy. (33) Re Moonchild: though I am sure it was instinctive at the time, my desire was for the images to be sort of Art Nouveau-ish. All Rossetti, Durer, Tiffanyesque and serpentine tendrils. The TV series "The Prisoner" was an influence on the first album. (34)

Michael Giles

AK: Who were your main musical influences in terms of drumming?

MG: Elvin Jones, Tony Williams and Tony Oxley.

AK: Did you know any of McLaughlin's work? I ask because Tony Oxley plays on that.

MG: Extrapolation was an extraordinary album and I was listening to all this stuff around the time of ITCOTCK. Duke Ellington was another influence as well as the free-jazz of John Stevens and the Spontaneous Music Ensemble. I used to go down to Ronnie Scott's and hear them. It was extraordinary. Bob Dylan was also a very strong influence, not so much musically but as a force who came onto the scene. Before that we'd had the likes of Presley and so on, but Dylan cut through like a knife through butter. It came from Blonde on Blonde. I wasn't so much interested in all his early acoustic music. I thought if Dylan can be a radical with his voice, I can be a radical with the drums. The Beatles' Sgt Pepper was also an inspiration. (35)

Greg Lake

A.K.: You mentioned that you felt you and Robert were central in the music that came into being for the first KC. However, Ian McDonald and Peter Sinfield appeared to be the main writing team. Perhaps they were the writing team, and you and Robert were the catalysts in defining the musical vision for the band?

G.L.: With regard to the writing it is very hard to generalise as it happens in so many different ways for so many different reasons. Contrasting elements were introduced by the various individuals concerned and in that sense it was a very collaborative effort. As far as the vision was concerned this evolved as a result of what everyone brought to the table. Robert was of course very technical, Ian and Pete were poetic, Mike contributed the rhythmical originality and I think that I introduced an overall rock sensibility and emotional passion to the writing. However this is only a very surface description of how the various pieces came about. Basically everybody had a role to play and in that sense everyone played an important part in the writing and creative process. Improvisation did play an important part in the live performance but less so in the writing.

A.K.: Was the writing a collective process? (i.e. did final pieces emerge from improvisation?)

G.L.: As above.

A.K.: Was it the same writing process in ELP?

G.L.: The writing process in ELP was different in the sense that it was pretty much Keith and I together that formed the basis of the writing partnership. Pete did come on occasions and when this happened there were obvious similarities to the way in which the material of KC was originated. Pete and I had a very close writing relationship and of course we understood each other very well because of our past experiences with KC.

A.K.: Who were your musical influences and what bearing might they have had on KC?

G.L.: Far too many to name. I think that most artists are influenced by almost everybody and everything in one way or another.

A.K.: Are you a classical guitarist by trade? I'm assuming this to be the case?

G.L.: No, my initial musical background on guitar was more early 20th century modern classics and early rock and roll. Robert and I went to the same guitar teacher (Don Strike) and often rehearsed our guitar lessons together at Robert's house in Wimborne when we were very young lads. Robert also often used to travel with me and my band at the time to various shows all over the country and this was really the very first exposure to rock music that Robert had. In that regard it was the fist meaningful musical relationship that was established in KC. Because we went to the same guitar teacher and used to practice together Robert and I had a very deep understanding of each others playing styles and musical knowledge and hence I believe that this was an important component in the music of KC. All of this of course happened long before Ian and Pete Sinfield arrived on the scene and of course before Mike and Pete Giles were involved as well.

A.K.: In retrospect, how do you view KC Mk I from a musical point of view?

G.L.: I think that the original King Crimson was a kind of phenomenon. It was undoubtedly inspired by the times in which we lived, but equally we were clearly on a mission to break new ground. In that sense we were consciously progressive.

A.K.: Which musicians of 'standing' appeared in the audience at early KC concerts?

G.L.: All sorts of people came to see KC all the way from Hendrix to the Moody Blues. However the band was not in existence for long so if you blinked you missed it.

A.K.: Do you think KC Mk I were the centre of the new, emerging London underground (1969)? Did it surprise you that KC Mk I had such enormous impact at the time and into the future?

G.L.: I think that KC was identified with the underground movement although this was more or less unintentional. It was really just who we were. No effort was ever made to really promote any sort of image or attach the band to any particular genre.

A.K.: Have you ever regretted leaving KC?

G.L.: I really didn't leave KC. The group came to an end when Ian and Mike left and I didn't feel that it was right to continue on with the band using the same name etc. without them. Perhaps if only one member had left I would have felt better about replacing them and continuing on but two people really was a bridge too far.

(Email correspondence between Greg Lake and the author, Dec. 2008).

6. Music Of The Period

I will go on to list some of the musics which precede and are contemporary with ITCOTCK which Fripp, McDonald, Sinfield and Giles have mentioned, and provide some brief notes about them. The music will not be listed chronologically.

Rock

The Yardbirds - Still I'm Sad (45 rpm single, 1965)
The Yardbirds were fronted by Keith Relf (vocals) and Jim McCarty (drums) both subsequently forming Renaissance. The Yardbirds' Still I'm Sad explores a quasi-Gregorian chant as a ritornello section within a two verse structure, where the chorus is connected to the Gregorian music. More importantly, it includes the Minor 9th chords found in The Court of the Crimson King, which also involves a chant-like section as a prelude to the verse.

Moody Blues - Days of Future Passed (1967)
A narrative about the passing of a day. Dvorak's New World Symphony is partially reworked during this. Use of mellotron,

classical structures and long harmonic rhythms. Dawn is a Feeling has a similar vocal delivery (from 0:38 to 1:52) to Greg Lake's on Epitaph but, more particularly, on Lake's The Endless Enigma from ELP's Tarkus (1971). The words sometimes fall slightly after the downbeat with upper grace-notes on some of the upper-range pitches. Subtitles to song names are used and, essentially, it is a concept album. Ballad-like song structures.

Love - Da Capo (1967)
Use of harpsichord, saxophone and flute in a band context. Irrational metres explored in Stephanie Knows Who, along with chromatic riffs at 0:59 and a wailing saxophone part reminiscent of some of Ian McDonald's playing. Flute included on Orange Skies. The Castle approaches the multi-sectional structures of some Progressive rock. There is a classical music input. Revelation is a very long song/piece at 18:57 and includes harpsichord, guitar, saxophone and bass guitar solos. J.S. Bach quotation at the beginning played on harpsichord as a prelude into the shuffle rhythm in some gestural guitar phrases as opposed to modal lines

Pretty Things - S.F. Sorrow (1967)
Example of the gradual transition from Psychedelic to Progressive. S.F. Sorrow was one of three albums recorded in the summer of 1967 at Abbey Road (i.e. Sgt. Pepper's Lonely Hearts Club Band; Piper at the Gates of Dawn; S.F. Sorrow.) S.F. Sorrow is a concept album featuring overlapping tracks. Probably known as the first rock opera. Includes anti-war songs and uses mellotron. I See You includes the Romanesca-like descending bass line: E Minor9 - D Major - A Major - B Major which was to become an important fingerprint in Progressive rock. The album was engineered by Norman Smith who also worked on Sgt. Pepper and Piper at the Gates of Dawn.

Pink Floyd - Piper at the Gates of Dawn (1967)
A huge influence on the Psychedelic and Progressive rock movements. Lucifer Sam includes a riff reminiscent of TV soundtracks (Mission Impossible etc). Improvisations and electronics are crucially important to the period mainly because of the associations with the distortion of temporality found in Psychedelia, and Pink Floyd were central to the *gesamtkunstwerk* of the late Psychedelic and Progressive rock bands of the period. Also Bike, probably following the example of

The Beatles, initiates the idea of a humorous song on Progressive rock albums from this time onwards. Texturally, especially with reference to keyboards, the album cannot be underestimated for its influence on later Progressive bands. Lyrically it is important for its use of mystical texts such as the I Ching (Chapter 24), the occult (Lucifer Sam), fairytale (Matilda Mother and The Gnome) and acid and sci-fi (Astronomy Domine). Engineered by Norman Smith.

The Beatles - Sgt. Pepper's Lonely Hearts Club Band (1967)

Cited as one of the great landmarks in popular music. The album, as a whole, deals with loneliness, isolation and imaginary states of mind and is designed as a show. If The Beatles were off the road they would make sure that they would take their show into listeners' front rooms in vinyl format in the form of a recorded show/circus. Broadly speaking, it is a concept album, including both serious and humorous elements which are held in balance, and instruments associated with classical music are to be heard throughout. Indian music is also accessed in the pedal pitch of Getting Better as well as in the sitar and tablas heard on Within You, Without You. Being for the Benefit of Mr. Kite points forward to King Crimson's Big Top on Lizard. The structure of the album is roughly symmetrical with the Sgt. Pepper reprise heard as a recapitulation. The multisectional A Day in the Life serves as a lengthy and powerful coda.

The Electric Prunes - I Had Too Much To Dream Last Night (1967)

A Psychedelic, fuzz guitar-driven band. The title track includes oscillating fifths in the bass guitar also heard in The Return of the Fire Witch from ITCOTCK. Fuzz guitar timbre is also used inside the texture, as found in the ritornelli and final section of ITCOTCK. IHTMTDLN includes orchestral instruments and chromatic sequences of early Barrett-led Pink Floyd. Try Me On For Size includes changes of metre from 4/4 - 6/8, and Sold to the Highest Bidder, besides its Russian musical influence, includes a i - bVII - bVI - V bass line. The album includes coded political messages. Try Me On For Size has a chromatic descent (0:34) similar to the opening of Moonchild.

Love - Forever Changes (1968)

Forever Changes has a timeless quality. Textures include 12-

string guitar. Alone Again Or includes Minor 9th chords (0:48ff), similar to those found on Epitaph. Strings are also used. This ends with acoustic guitar alone, which is similar to the end of Exiles on the King Crimson's later Larks' Tongues in Aspic. Phrygian harmonic shifts found in The Red Telephone at 1:24 - Bb4 - A (9-8 susp).

Iron Butterfly - In-A-Gadda-Da-Vida (1968)
Some Baroque-like counterpoint in the organ part (Iron Butterfly's leader, Doug Ingle, says his father was a church organist) of Most Anything You Want. Many examples of Major seventh chords. Guitar timbre and guitar and organ arrangements important at the time. Wind-chimes included in Termination. Drum sound similar in places to that found on ITCOTCK i.e. very muted. Title-track is 17:05 in duration.

Jimi Hendrix - Are You Experienced? (1967)
A soul/blues/rock album of great character transcending its time. The riff from Foxy Lady was important for a song, Brightness Falls, on the later Sylvian/Fripp collaboration, The First Day. Hendrix came to England to experience first-hand the English approach to electric blues by Cream and, especially, Eric Clapton. Riff-based music with guitar and 'noise' is at the centre of the album. It has a very fluid and economical style and is central to the *zeitgeist*. Hendrix was able to play three parts seemingly at once (rhythm, fills and lead) and probably did for rock what Miles Davis did for jazz. Hendrix, along with Cream, gave voice to electric blues within the counter-culture by popularising the genre. Third Stone from the Sun is LSD-inspired, combining jazz and an Eastern approach within a rock format. Improvisation is at the core of this modal ostinati. The 45-rpm single, Purple Haze, includes powerful angular leaps in the guitar solo and the 'head' is played around an E Minor7 chord with pull-offs to open strings. The central guitar solo is Eastern in flavour and uses parallel octaves. The opening E/Bb tritones had a particular bearing on Fripp's developing style.

The Beatles - Double White Album (1968)
A reaction to the Sgt. Pepper album of the previous year. An eclectic album (country music - Rocky Raccoon; rock n'roll - Back in the USSR; acoustic - Blackbird; musique concrete - Revolution No. 9; regional music hall - Honey Pie; orchestral - Good Night) and self-referential with psychedelic subjects and humour still

prevalent. It has a greater input from John Lennon, as compared to Sgt. Pepper, but Paul McCartney continues to provide lyricism while the album is more a collection of songs and experiments. Many examples of descending ostinato bass lines in songs such as Dear Prudence and While My Guitar Gently Weeps.

Frank Zappa and the Mothers of Invention - We're Only In It For The Money (1968)

A send-up of the hippie dream and, especially, The Beatles' Sgt. Pepper, even down to the sleeve design. Who Needs the Peace Corps is the quintessential cynical take on the counter-culture focussing on the hypocrisy of the hippies. Multi-sectional and employing many different styles (such as The Beach Boys) to make its point.

Folk and Country

Bob Dylan - various

The Freewheelin' Bob Dylan (1963) includes the epic Blowin' in the Wind. Dylan suggested that the way to answer the questions posed in the song was to first find the wind. It is, essentially, an anti-war protest album which works a kind of catharsis in a listener after repeated listening. Hard Rain, for example, was written during the Cuban Missile Crisis of 1962. Folk music, with its unhindered accompaniment of acoustic instruments, offered an authentic mouthpiece for performers who wished to present important social truths for listeners to hear with great clarity.

Blonde on Blonde (1966) was the definitive 'electric' Dylan album and includes the epic Sad Eyed Lady of the Lowlands, a love song for his wife, Sara.

John Wesley Harding (1967) includes All Along the Watchtower, later covered by Jimi Hendrix. The lyrics of this song seem to have been an influence on Peter Sinfield's allegorical subjects. One of the first songs to use a harmony which, subsequently, became a cliché for some of the Progressive rock bands: i - bVII - bVI, three-quarters of the descending Romanesca bass-line mentioned previously.

Donovan - Fairy Tale (1965)
Fairy Tale, as I have already written, was a quintessential influence on Peter Sinfield. Catch the Wind is, in a sense, distantly related to Bob Dylan's Blowin' in the Wind which is, in turn, related to I Talk to the Wind from ITCOTCK.

Fairport Convention - Fairport Convention (1968)
This album has great delicacy with a light jazz influence. The opening of The Lobster (0:00 - 0:10) has a direct bearing on the opening of the improvisation of Moonchild from ITCOTCK. Judy Dyble's experience in the Fairports had an impact on the music of Giles, Giles and Fripp II. Ian McDonald owns the first Fairports album and 'often listens to it.' (36) Sun Shade is close to the atmosphere of some of Giles, Giles and Fripp's material and its harmony and axial melody at 0:34 in Db is close to Make It Today on Giles, Giles and Fripp's The Brondesbury Tapes

Donovan - A Gift from a Flower to a Garden (1968)
A jazz/folk counter-cultural statement plus green issues and flower-power and fairytale-like imagery. Presented love and knowledge of 'inner' realms to the counter-culture. It also conveys Buddhist precepts, as well as being a celebration of the earth. Donovan had been, at this time, introduced to the meditation techniques of the Maharishi. It is also an anti-drugs album and its sleevenotes convey this message. Lyrics are colourful, both Eastern and Romantic. Wear Your Love Like Heaven includes a Phrygian chord shift (Eb Major to D Minor) at 0:33 which is close to the coda of Epitaph on ITCOTCK. The song also includes vibraphone and flute which also reappear on Oh Gosh.

The Incredible String Band - The Hangman's Beautiful Daughter (1968)
An album of stories and poetry of a mythical kind which found its place within the counter-culture. A Very Cellular Song is multisectional with irrational metres. Combines traditional folk music with world music and classical music on Witches Hat.

Neil Young and Crazy Horse - Everybody Knows This Is Nowhere (1968)
Basically country blues, with tight three-part harmony vocals. A loose improvisational feel including many love songs.

Nick Drake - Five Leaves Left (1969)

A highly eclectic and subsequently influential album. Tim Buckley, Donovan, Bert Jansch and jazz/classical/world music influences are heard. Includes songs of great strength adorned with inspirational arrangements. Produced by Joe Boyd. (see www.andrewkeeling.ukf.net for three essays on the music of Nick Drake).

Jazz

Eric Dolphy - Out to Lunch (1964)

Album of post-Bebop pieces heard as a transition from the more stylised music of Miles Davis or Charlie Parker to the free-form/modal interests of jazz in the 1960's. Hat and Beard includes a partially whole-tone riff in 9/8 as the 'head' of the piece, dissonance throughout set in a symmetrical structure. Dolphy's bass clarinet playing utilises small and sudden gestures as part of the phrasing with angular intervals. The structural symmetry is close to 21st Century Schizoid Man. Modal riffing, in the hands of players such as Dolphy, was an important component in the vocabulary of players such as Miles Davis and John Coltrane. Dolphy's band, at this time, also included Freddie Hubbard (trumpet), Bobby Hutcherson (vibes) and Tony Williams (drums).

John Handy - Live at the Monterey Jazz Festival (1965)

Ian McDonald has said John Handy is one of the most important influences on his saxophone playing. 'I loved the way that Handy would play little phrases ending up with shrieking high notes, and the way he'd break out of the ensemble to be left playing solo.' (37) Moments such as this can be heard on King Crimson's Live in Hyde Park 1969 (DGM Club 12) in Get Thy Bearings from 2:11ff. Live at Monterey also includes similar moments during If Only We Knew at 21:37. There is much playing over modal ostinati rather than walking chromatic bass lines which anticipates the vocabulary found in some jazz rock. Jerry Hahn's guitar playing includes the half-bends heard in some of Robert Fripp's earlier playing and, especially, the rapid right-hand tremolos at 13:33 of If Only We Knew. Hahn also uses techniques such as rapid cross-picking at 14:02. This solo, in particular, is striking for its influence on later Fripp solos in the context King Crimson I. The second piece, Spanish Lady, is perhaps even more telling in terms of a possible influence on the first King Crimson. The piece has a drone underpinning the dynamic energy. It also includes fast unison riffs in 6/8 reminiscent of those found in Schizoid Man, and the passage at 9:33, with its pentatonic minor, is identical to the 0-3-5-7-5-3 riffs heard in Mirrors, one of the subsection choruses, of Schizoid Man. The Minor third tremolandos in the saxophone part at 12:26 is also a feature of McDonald's technique. Handy's band also use extreme dynamics as part of the structure. The 'head' of pieces is also segued into the choruses. The music of Spanish Lady has other farther-reaching influences. For example, David Cross' 'live' improvisations during Larks' Tongues In Aspic period King Crimson III is close to some of Mike White's playing on Live at Monterey. Fripp's playing also seems to have been affected by Hahn in terms of the sul ponticelli tremolandos heard at 14:21 of Spanish Lady, which also may have been taken into the introduction of The Nightwatch (Starless and Bible Black - 1973).

John McLaughlin - Extrapolation (1969)
Free-form jazz-rock including the impressive line-up of McLaughlin (guitar), John Surman (saxes), Brian Odges (bass) and Tony Oxley (drums). It's Funny includes the Phrygian bVI - V harmonies found on Epitaph and Eastern-like modal lines. Some of the album is reminiscent, in places, of King Crimson's subsequent In the Wake of Poseidon.

In brief, other possible influences on the members of King Crimson:

Tim Buckley - Happy Sad (1969), Soft Machine I (1968), The Doors - Waiting for the Sun (1968), Procul Harum - Shine On Brightly (1968), Captain Beefheart and his Magic Band - Troutmask Replica (1969), Colosseum - Valentyne Suite (1969), Wes Montgomery - Movin' Wes (1964), Tal Farlow - The Swinging Guitar of Tal Farlow (1956), John Coltrane - A Love Supreme (1964), Miles Davis - Kind of Blue (1959), Spontaneous Music Ensemble - Withdrawal (1966/67).

7. The Counter-culture and Zeitgeist of the 1960's

The revolution of the 1960's was different from others. The decade was colourful, emerging as the result of the upturn in economies in Europe and America following World War II. It brought with it an optimism coupled with the liberation of several ethnic and other minority groups throughout the West. Intellectuals such as Timothy Leary and Richard Alpert promoted Eastern influences as a discipline for personal change and transformation, feeding into the counter-cultural explosion as a means of liberation from the status-quo through the use of drugs, meditation and other Eastern techniques. At the centre of this revolution, pioneered by middle-class youth culture, was an ethos of peace and the transformation of the 'inner' man or woman as a way to affect the collective psyche. Its symbol was the flower, signifying a return to the natural world, and through this can be seen a reaction to the industrial, over-urbanised modern environment.

The summer of 1967 saw the counter-culture in direct conflict with establishment law enforcement agencies both in Europe and in the USA. The main thrust of this was reflected in the music of

Bob Dylan initially regarded as a mouthpiece for the Civil Rights Movement of the early 1960's and, alongside The Beatles and Jimi Hendrix, for the counter-culture itself. Students, and other minority groups, had been awakened to the hypocrisy of the establishment largely through the horrors of the Vietnam War witnessed first-hand by millions on TV screens throughout the world. As a result, alternative modes of living were sought after. Indeed, the youth generation questioned real and illusory states, something which fed directly into their artworks. The middle classes primed the cultural revolution, and rock music became the dominant form of expression railing against positions of authority such as governments, police, teachers and parents. The music and lyrics of the period epitomise the position taken by, mainly, white middle-class youth. The upturn in the economy also meant the young had more money at their disposal to spend on activities of which the arts figured highly. Greater financial freedom also meant wider choices for the individual, and the greater the polarisation in hegemonies giving rise to dominant subcultures, the greater the variety of bricolage emerged, sonic or otherwise.

The '60's flower children were the first subculture to promote 'happenings' and festivals at which they could gather and spread their gospel of change by passive means. Music featured prominently. Robert Fripp: '...In the 1960's young people believed that simply by listening one could make a difference... there was a particular *zeitgeist*. We believed that music could change the world, and that we could have effect in the world. Idries Shah once told J.G. Bennett that the creative powers (or muse or however we might characterise this) invested energy in the large festivals. Mr. Bennett went to the Isle-of-Wight to check this out. My own sense, and part of this is from my experience of King Crimson from 1969-74, is that there was a download of creative energy that went into popular music at the time. The Beatles shared a common genius, and it didn't belong to any of them. It continues to reverberate. Dylan and Hendrix were also part of this current. I believe that King Crimson were at the end of the download.' (38)

The term *zeitgeist* may loosely be termed 'spirit of the age'. C.G. Jung has said that the word spirit stands in opposition to matter by which we understand an immaterial substance or form of existence. (39) Equally common is the view that spirit and psyche is essentially the same. Jung also mentions the spirit of the age, which stands for the principle and motive behind certain views, judgements, and actions of a collective nature. The 'objective spirit' is meant as the whole stock of man's cultural possessions. Associated with the term *zeitgeist* as applied to 1960's culture, I believe there is some connection with Jung's definition of spirit that is 'in keeping with its original wind-nature, spirit is always an active, winged, swift-moving being as that which vivifies, stimulates, incites, fires and inspires. To put it in modern language, spirit is the dynamic principle....the classical antithesis of matter...its invisible presence is a psychic phenomenon...its synonym the soul, that glancing Aeolian thing, evasive as a butterfly'. (40) Indeed, '...it is the descent of spirit into matter as expressed in the myth of the divine Nous caught in the embrace of Physis' (in Gnosticism). Man did not create the spirit, rather the spirit makes him creative...giving him lucky ideas, staging power, enthusiasm and inspiration.' (41) Perhaps this sums up the mysterious dynamism associated with the counter-culture, where a vibrant 'scene' was created to fight unjust causes at all costs.

Michael Giles has spoken of Bob Dylan in terms of possessing a 'universal knowledge': 'Dylan was a twentieth century poet. He couldn't have learned and experienced all this stuff. He must have had a leaking umbrella for universal knowledge. Some people are more open to this than others. The great composers are a case in point and Dylan also had a dose of it. Maybe if someone gets too large a dose of this universal outpouring it leads to a down and out overload! It's true that King Crimson may have suffered from its effects. However, if you connect with this universal knowledge in a genuine and human way it might present you with a certain truth because it is organic and wholesome. Music is infinite with no ending. Organic music has a sense of identity - Dylan, Joni Mitchell, for example, if you want the real thing. They have invented this unique signature.' (42) A telling line from Jung perhaps puts the term spirit into perspective: '...Objective spirit did not mean the universal spirit, or God, but merely the sum total of intellectual and cultural perceptions which make up our human institutions and the content of our libraries. Spirit had forfeited its original nature.' (43) In Gurdjieffian/J.G. Bennett cosmology, this is represented by a movement from World VI to World XXII.

I believe the *zeitgeist* of the 1960's was a gradual dawning of consciousness which began much earlier, perhaps even as far back as the eighteenth century with J. J. Rousseau's view of the 'noble savage' and his championing of the free and natural in children and adults alike. The world of nature and the imagination are central to an understanding of this, possibly as a response to the Industrial Revolution. Partially, this was a reaction to the earlier Reformation and is the moral outcome of the Age of Enlightenment. William Blake's observation of the shackles imposed by eighteenth century authority is also well known in this context. Romanticism, particularly in the agenda of the Lakes poets, may be seen as a culmination of the attitudes of both Rousseau and Blake. Wordsworth's view of a spirit within nature in Intimations of Immortality can be read literally or as a metaphorical reaction to the Cumbrian landscape. Coleridge's work, however, opens this up to the world of the interior as an inscape, observed in his poem, Kublah Khan. Keats and ultimately the Pre-Raphaelites resume Wordsworth's ethos and find voice in John Ruskin whose love of nature and the understanding of the arts are closely interwoven. Ruskin writes: '...throughout the history of this wonderful art...sculpture founded on love of nature, was the talisman for existence...Gothic is not an art for knights and nobles; it is an art for the people; it is not an art for churches or sanctuaries; it is not an art for houses and homes; it is not an art for England only, but an art for the world; above all it is not an art of form or tradition only, but an art of vital practice and perpetual renewal...whoever pleads for it as an ancient or a formal thing and tried to teach it...as an ecclesiastical tradition or a geometric science, knows nothing of its essence, less nothing of its power...Thus then, you will find... that the living power in all the real schools, be they great or small, is love of nature.' (44)

The world of the imagination is, for Blake, the experience of Jesus himself. For Keats and Shelley, nature, imagination and the notion of art for art's sake are synonymous and all important. Their work is based on mythical deities within nature - perhaps remnants of alchemical precepts - the idealisation of the medieval and the sensuously descriptive. The outworking of this interest in nature eventually finds its way into the paintings of John Constable, alerting the beholder to nature in all its wildness and diversity. Themes found in Shelley and Keats resurface in Tennyson's The Lady of Shalott, and the Pre-Raphaelite painters

(Dante Gabriel Rossetti, William Morris and Edward Burne-Jones) offered works with clear detail and colouring, creating a medieval world of knights, fair maidens, castles and questers. Keats invests these themes with modern, secular and erotic spirit with a ready-made territory of the imagination. In turn such poetic medievalism generated many distinctive features of Victorian architecture - ecclesiastical, bureaucratic and industrial. (45)

Nature eventually resurfaces in the musical works of the New English Renaissance in the works of Vaughan-Williams, Arnold Bax and Peter Warlock together with a smattering of esotericism via Holst's The Hymn of Jesus and The Planets. Connected with these are the occult interests of The Order Of The Golden Dawn, whose membership included Aleister Crowley (whose novel Moonchild is notable), W.B. Yeats, Dion Fortune and William McGregor Mathers. The Golden Dawn was also connected to such occult groups as The Men of Trees. Peter Sinfield: 'My grandfather 'Beak' was a member of The Men of Trees together with my wooden-legged, great aunt, the author Mable Lethbridge, were both on the fringes of Notting Hill bohemian circles which probably included various members of The Golden Dawn. There was also Maria Wallenda (the high-wire walker) who was part of our household for some years. Circus folk are often on the darkling side of the superstitious.' (46) Sinfield has also said that the 'occult was a part of the *zeitgeist* of the time, for in certain "hip" circles, to which I was close, explaining with the use of substances various, Casteneda, The Tibetan Book of the Dead and The Doors of Perception.' (47)

The influence of folksong not only found its way into art music. It was also taken up by the Protest Movement by way of Ewan McColl and Peggy Seeger and was hugely popularised by Bob Dylan in the USA and Donovan in the UK. At the back end of the 1960's this became the folk rock movement pioneered by the likes of Fairport Convention and Steeleye Span. These many undercurrents invest the new rock music of the late '60's with an incredible diversity in the form of Progressive rock but, more specifically, the 'fantastic' which I will discuss later.

Jazz was also central to the Beatnik generation of the late 1950's spilling over into the 1960's. By 1948, the Bebop era in jazz had attracted many of the new players into its vortex. Such players as

Charlie Parker are synonymous with the movement, and in 1959 Ornette Coleman ushered in the genre known as free-jazz with the sensational The Shape of Jazz to Come. There was a strong ideological undercurrent at the time with the passage of the Civil Rights Act (1957), and the demonstrations and beatings and eventual arrest of Dr. Martin Luther King, following landmark legislation and the Voting Rights Act (1965). Many black musicians were envigorated by the atmosphere of the time and Sonny Rollins recorded his Freedom Suite which symbolised, for some, the arrival of a new era. (48)

However, free-jazz exacerbated the downswing of the popularity of jazz as a whole. Rock music was seen as the culprit and jazz clubs closed as people began to dance to the new rock n'roll. Artists such as Duke Ellington started to record songs by The Beatles and, in 1967, Woody Herman performed a jazz-rock piece at the Monterey Jazz Festival. Players and composers such as Eric Dolphy and John Handy had clearly signalled the shape of things to come with their albums Out to Lunch and Live at Monterey. In 1962 jazz and rock eventually merged in the UK via Alexis Korner. The blues boom of the 1960's was another vital ingredient in the *zeitgeist* and Korner combined both styles employing musicians such as Dick Heckstall Smith, later of Colosseum, in his band. Blues Incorporated emerged from this, which included Jack Bruce, Ginger Baker, John McLaughlin and Graham Bond, which in turn gave rise to the Graham Bond Organisation from which Bruce was eventually to leave to form Cream with ex-John Mayall's Bluesbreakers guitarist Eric Clapton. From these beginnings arose many of the blues-rock bands of the late 1960's such as Led Zeppelin and Free who, along with Black Sabbath and Deep Purple, were the pioneers of what has become known broadly as metal. It is also worth mentioning bands such as Colosseum and Soft Machine were acquainted with the music of European avant-garde composers such as Karlheinz Stockhausen, Luciano Berio and Pierre Boulez.

Keith Tippett and John Surman are musicians who were playing a series of concerts at the Marquee in June 1969 entitled New Paths, and are perhaps the British response to the free-jazz coming from the US. Tippett's I Am There...You Are Here (1968) is a suite that draws on rock and jazz. John Surman was to eventually play on John McLaughlin's Extrapolation (1969). King Crimson were also part of the New Paths residency. It is clear from early 'live' recordings of King Crimson that they were, without doubt, part of this collective *zeitgeist* in terms of the many diverse undercurrents I have discussed. King Crimson go beyond the vocabulary of jazz-rock because of their incorporation of classical sonorities in the form of mellotron (Epitaph and The Court of the Crimson King), by drawing on folksong-like musics (I Talk to the Wind) and rock music (the 'head' of Schizoid Man). This synthesis of styles, something revolutionary at the time, defined the Progressive rock music that was to follow in its wake with bands such as Genesis, Yes, Van der Graaf Generator, T2, Renaissance etc.

Modernism and Postmodernism are as much part of the *zeitgeist* as is the return to nature approach which I have previously discussed. It could be claimed that Modernism began with the Industrial Revolution and the growth of technology. However, culturally it is often thought that the Modernist paradigm was initiated by Debussy, Satie and Koechlin as a reaction to the Austro-German symphonic repertoire with smaller, more lightweight works. Debussy and the French Symbolist poets influenced Arnold Schoenberg who turned mainly to chamber works based on text settings and instrumental works imbued with the atmosphere of the Berlin cabaret and Freudian psychoanalysis. Schoenberg's early, Expressionistic style dictated by the angst of the personal subconscious, gradually became more disciplined with the advent of his, and Hauer's, experiments with serialism. Serialism, greatly refined in the works of Schoenberg's student Anton Webern, passed to the younger generation of composers such as Olivier Messiaen, Pierre Boulez and Karlheinz Stockhausen before being adapted by such composers as Milton Babbit in the USA, and Peter Maxwell Davies and David Lumsdaine in the UK. Musical modernism aims for transcendence and seeks an escape from what Theodor Adorno saw as the vulgarity of the culture industry by avoiding tonal harmony and traditional melody. The rhythmic energy found in Stravinsky's early primitivist ballets is curbed by serial techniques in later works such as In Memoriam Dylan Thomas. In Modernist literature the poet e.e.cummings and the writer James Joyce sought to transform the dimension of temporality, whilst Virginia Woolf's To the Lighthouse relates the events of one day in a stream-of-consciousness style. In the fine arts, Kandinsky and Klee pointed to Theosophical modes of expression as a way of reaching the sublime.

Postmodernism was a reaction to the Modernist paradigm admitting a playfulness and a polystylism, quotations from historical styles in the form of pastiche, eclecticism and the decentering of works by creating fictions and pluralism. Musical works, such as those by Alfred Schnittke, epitomise this tendency. For example, his Fifth Symphony not only quotes an unfinished Piano Quartet by Gustav Mahler, but also includes a Baroque Concerto as its first movement before semi-quoting Mahler's Der Abschied, from Das Lied von der Erde, going on to pastiche Mahler's style in the remaining three movements. This form of juxtaposition is common in Postmodern musical styles. Other Postmodern composers are George Rochberg, whose String Quartet No. 3 juxtaposes Mahler-like material within a style close to Beethoven. Perhaps the American, Charles Ives, was the first to admit widescale borrowings in his works from sources as diverse as hymn tunes and marching bands in a style which may be described as montage.

It seems to me that ITCOTCK stands between these two 'isms', by seeking transcendence but simultaneously utilising many influences from diverse sources to make its 'observations' all the more powerful and pertinent for the culture with which it sought to communicate. It stands as the post-Dylan, post-Beatles counter-cultural sonic pamphlet par excellence.

8. Protest and Strategy

King Crimson's strategy was a simple one born of innocence and ambition: 'to be the best band in the world.' (49) I believe that their strategy was one partly inspired by Brian Epstein's vision for The Beatles which involved transition from local to regional and then national popularity. Looking at this aspect might be important in decoding why the music of the band, and especially ITCOTCK, developed in the way it did.

As with The Beatles, King Crimson developed a marketable and unique sound, look and story allying themselves to the DIY counter-cultural techniques of advertising. This was as a direct reaction against establishment forms of marketing. For example, Sid Smith notes that to help get the buzz going, the band had 100 posters printed, designed by their friend Barry Godber (a friend of Peter Sinfield's who was also responsible for the cover paintings on the sleeve of ITCOTCK) which McDonald and Sinfield fly-posted along the King's Road and other strategic locations around the city (50). In other words, they geared their message to the politically active anti-establishment sectors of the counter-culture which is also reflected in Fripp's letter to the International Times: 'The fundamental aim of King Crimson is to organise anarchy, to utilise the latent power of chaos and to allow the varying influences to interact and find their own equilibrium. The music, therefore, naturally evolves rather than develops along predetermined lines. The widely differing repertoire has a common theme in that it represents the changing moods of the same five people.' (51) Fripp also comments, 'Chris Welch (a music journalist active from the 1960's to the 1980's) thought the Hyde Park concert marked the end of an era in music. If it ended the...sounds of the '60's perhaps it augured in the music of the '70's, which would seem to be a music that is more self-conscious than before to the degree that...different forms are sought, ones which expect a reaction from the head rather than the foot.' (52) Fripp's comment is particularly relevant to the then emerging Progressive rock style, which I will discuss later. Indeed, press coverage of the band during this period, as every subsequent period in which King Crimson have been operational, was widely divided in its opinions about the band.

Having secured management in the form of David Enthoven and John Gaydon and a financial advance from Angus Hunking (Ian McDonald's step-uncle), they groped around for what was best for themselves, largely taking control of their own collective destiny. Fripp: 'My own view, as a beginning professional, was that if I worked hard enough for long enough a measure of professional success would inevitably follow...Angus Hunking was a good man. He told us he could afford to lose £7,000 without prejudicing his retirement, but not more. He didn't believe he would see any of it back and was probably very surprised when he did (after the break-up of KCI in 1969). He would not have sued us had we failed, as he likely expected. E&G came from the Noel Gay office (Giles, Giles and Fripp management), were going independent and expressed an interest in Giles, Giles and Fripp before it became the nascent King Crimson. Once the penny dropped with them that King Crimson was a winner (one week into rehearsals) everything changed. At that point, realistic strategies came into play - something was possible. My own expectation, at the very beginning and before many rehearsals, was that King Crimson would earn a living playing the music that was there for us to play, and we would earn that living because we'd play it well; but I didn't anticipate the level of success that found us. Until a few weeks into rehearsals...the responses from visitors to rehearsals were exceptionally positive. And then the early performances... .' (53)

So as to validate their message the band took well-known styles and genres - jazz (Schizoid Man), folk (I Talk to the Wind), classical symphonic 'hymn' (Epitaph), Renaissance-like/free-form improvisation (Moonchild), rock 'anthem' (The Court of the Crimson King) - to develop the ultimate post-Dylan, grand-slam form of sonic protest. In taking their destiny into their own hands, King Crimson both changed the contemporary music scene and were themselves transformed by the implosion which finally overcame them. The paradigm was to quickly collapse. Perhaps King Crimson's approach owed something to The Beatles' with their Apple records project, which also imploded mainly because they found it impossible to be creative and to deal with business simultaneously. However, in following the paradigm, King Crimson also created a synthesis with the ongoing model that Fripp and Sinfield adopted during the subsequent 'interregnum' period of eighteen months, where the band became, to all intents and purposes, a recording rather than a gigging band. The paradigm has also continued to the present day with Fripp's formation of his own record company, Discipline Global Mobile, and DGM Live!

King Crimson Mk I existed before the cynicism of today's marketing strategies had rendered the concept of experimentation an irritating and potentially destructive nuisance. Fripp: 'This was a groundbreaking approach from EG. EG provided the finance so the record (ITCOTCK) was our property not the label's (Island Records). The implosion is much more detailed than this. Mainly, this is a record of personal failings. Partly, it has to do with large amounts of money pouring into EG. The young managers used this for their own interests not King Crimson's.... Partly this has to do with some of the young men having their attention diverted from the creative process. Partly, this is because for them (one in particular) music was the way to "success" and its seductions rather than an aim in its own right. Partly, this is to do with the lack of personal discipline of those young men. Management and players were all young and had no experience in being very successful, and how to handle success and the pressures.... For me...something else came into the picture - music leant over and took us into its confidence. The power that is part of this is easily recognisable. It was this power that you (AK) recognised as a young man, and made the band successful. People felt the musical power, and I was one of them. The power was not the property of the young men - and it was made available to them as a gift. I don't believe they fully recognised this. What is required is, to hold the space that music might enter...' (54)

9. Progressive Rock

Edward Macan has observed, in his exhaustive study of Progressive rock - Rocking the Classics, English Progressive Rock and the Counter-culture - that the style emerged from Psychedelia merging with folk musics in the first wave of progressive bands, such as The Moody Blues, Procul Harum and Pink Floyd. He also writes, 'The release of King Crimson's... ITCOTCK in October 1969 signalled the emergence of the mature Progressive rock style, which reached its artistic and commercial zenith between 1970 and 1975 in the music of bands such as Jethro Tull, Yes, Genesis, ELP, Gentle Giant, Van der Graaf Generator and Curved Air.' (55) Macan makes the point that the conventions that govern the music are, essentially, centred on a *gesamtkunstwerk* - a unified work of art, and a term derived from nineteenth century composer Richard Wagner - to describe the equal importance of music, words, scenery, lighting and, even, costume design. These elements are inextricably intertwined so as to convey a coherent artistic vision. This vision encapsulates counter-cultural ideology: it simultaneously protests against the soulless bureaucracy which the youth of the age believed was crushing every trace of spiritual life from Western culture, and suggests an ideal, somewhat elitist society in which technology and nature, past and future, matriarchal and patriarchal social values could be harmoniously interwoven. (56)

I suggest that The Beatles accidentally began the Progressive rock movement with the concept of a 'live' show included in vinyl format, as a substitute for 'live' performance. Archie Loss has pointed out that Sgt. Pepper has a unity analogous to that which a poet might give to a volume of verse, or a painter to an exhibition of work. I have previously discussed some of the unifying elements in the lyrics of Sgt. Pepper: the emphasis on loneliness, the fear of separation or allusions to drugs and drug experience. The more complex lyrics owe a debt to Bob Dylan's, and the songs depended on effects which could be achieved only in the studio which, in turn, owed a great deal to Phil Spector's 'wall of sound' (57)

In Progressive rock, particularly during its first phase, it is possible to discern a growing concern for large-scale musical structures, and the song Sgt. Pepper's Lonely Hearts Club Band, with its recurrence of the opening song at the end, has the effect of providing the album with a cyclical structure of sorts. In short, Sgt. Pepper was generally recognised as the first concept album. (58) A key component of the Progressive style was also the use of a wide variety of instruments, whilst retaining the basic guitar, bass and drum textures crucial to rock. Bands experimented with virtuosity, and the organ was one of the first instruments to be emancipated from its traditional role as accompaniment into an instrument in its own right. Orchestral sonorities, in the form of the mellotron, and traditional classical music instruments were also added. These were the flute, oboe, clarinet, bass clarinet and violin, and even instruments associated with ethnic cultures like the sitar. New electronic effects were also introduced, such as phasing, and the new stereo effect was used to particularly striking effect (King Crimson's Catfood/Groon was the first 45-rpm single to be made in stereo). The Moog and VCS3 synthesisers were employed soloistically and to create new timbres. Macan has added that the multi-movement suite was introduced via the Psychedelic movement (59) and instrumental pieces attempted to convey an extramusical source of inspiration, perhaps in a similar way to that of the tone poem of the nineteenth century. The aim of sophistication was also extended to lyrics which, in effect, became large-scale song-cycles like Mahler's Das Lied von der Erde.

Macan observes that ITCOTCK 'had an especially powerful effect on the nascent Progressive rock movement, and just may be the most influential progressive rock album ever released...(it) displays every major element of the Progressive rock genre.' (60). Macan has developed this by saying that ITCOTCK 'crystallise(s) these elements into a distinctive, immediately recognisable style...Both its melancholy minor key passages permeated by acoustic guitar and the mellotron's symphonic colourings and its muscular, polyrhythmic jazz-tinged stylisations dominated by alto sax and fuzzed guitar were to reverberate in Progressive rock throughout the 1970's. The album exerted a powerful extramusical influence on later Progressive rock bands as well: both the apocalyptic subject matter of Epitaph and Schizoid Man and the medieval imagery and mystical undertones of the title-track...greatly influenced later Progressive rock bands, as did the albums surrealistic gothic cover art.' (61) It is true that ITCOTCK inspired such bands as Yes and Genesis. It could also be argued that Progressive rock essentially retained the three-minute song extending it to include long instrumental episodes. Structure aside, the players from different bands became counter-cultural household names through their technical dexterity. Macan has also observed that the 'prototypical Progressive rock rhythm can...be regarded as a fusion of the steady beat and syncopated rhythms of African-American popular music (especially jazz) and the asymmetrical and shifting metres of European folk music mediated through the music of twentieth century nationalist composers such as Stravinsky, Bartok, Holst and Vaughan Williams.' (62) Combined with instrumental virtuosity, the multi-movement suite, the Tone Poem/ orchestral song-cycle, the extension of the three minute song, rhythm from various sources and classical harmony (modal or otherwise) gave the music 'a sense of monumentality and grandeur.' (63)

10. Fantasy and the world of Peter Sinfield

Ian McDonald has said that Peter Sinfield 'created the world of the fantastic with the lyrics of ITCOTCK. It was an imaginary landscape and he used it to comment on the establishment. It was a case of the "straights" versus the "heads", and it was also to do with the generation gap. It was designed as this kind of fantasy based on an awareness of what was going on at the time. Musically we took advantage of the moment. It was also thanks to The Beatles. They opened it up for musicians. They were the first Progressive rock band. Strings had been used before, in the case of Buddy Holly for example, but in Yesterday the fact there was a classical string quartet marked something new in pop music and that's when I recognised something new was opening up. The string quartet was essential.' (64)

As I have previously suggested, a line may be drawn back to the Romantic period of the eighteenth century which connects with the 1960's. This emphasis on nature and the 'invisible' world of the imagination was taken up by The Order of the Golden Dawn, via the repealing in 1951 of the Witchcraft Act of 1735, to the concept of the fantastic which first began to reappear in the music of the counter-culture of the mid to late '60's in the interest in works of such authors as J.R.R. Tolkien, Hermann Hesse, Mervyn Peake and Carlos Castaneda. Allan F. Moore has said: 'The private mythologies of Marc Bolan represent one aspect of the intrusion of the fantastic into Progressive rock. Fantasy is the style's only important non-musical source, but in many ways it is the most deeply influential. It takes many forms...King Crimson's ITCOTCK...the sources here are less science fiction than the epic fantasy and allegory of writers like Moorcock...Tolkien and Peake. Similar imagery can be found in bands as widely differentiated as ELP, The Strawbs, Led Zeppelin, Tyrannosaurus Rex...Clearly these types of imagery set such bands apart from the commercial end of the market with their concentration on obscure and occult...matters, their lack of obvious ways of looking at things...' (65) Moore elaborates saying that the fantastic in rock seems predicated upon Gnosis which are beliefs that salvation is gained by knowledge, and that obscurity is striven for since it intensifies the achievement of the goal. (66) Gnosis also provides initiates with perilous trials through which they must pass, and retains the 'secret' of what is sought and which must be kept from the masses. This is part of the listening process of Progressive rock bands; part of the coding through which listeners encounter in works such as ITCOTCK, In the Wake of Poseidon and Larks' Tongues in Aspic. Fairytale imagery, myth and fantasy are also related to Psychedelic experience to provide a related experience to the religious encounters found in Eastern religions. This is the dimension of 'immediate experience'. (67) In the works of some bands the unfamiliarity of free-jazz and aspects of fantasy were combined to enhance the sense of strangeness. Moore has suggested that the 'recourse to such imagery both for King Crimson and Van der Graaf Generator is tied to a rather "gothic" sense of impending doom.' (68)

I have already mentioned Peter Sinfield's influences in the form of Bob Dylan and Donovan, but there is also a line running from Dylan, through Donovan and eventually to Marc Bolan. It is well known that Donovan was initially marketed as the British answer to Bob Dylan, in much the same way that Cliff Richard was promoted as an anglicised version of Elvis Presley. It is also known that Donovan influenced Marc Bolan. Donovan was connected with the anti-war position of Dylan and Joan Baez, but on one or two of the songs from Fairytale and, particularly, on the later A Gift from a Flower to a Garden, the aims of the Peace movement become mixed-in with Psychedelia without recourse to drugs. Donovan is quite explicit in his stance on anti-drugs as exemplified by the sleeve-notes of A Gift from a Flower to a Garden. Indeed, Donovan's source of inspiration was, like The Beatles, from the Maharishi Yogi - the famed 1960's guru - and Transcendental Meditation: in other words, altered states of consciousness by natural means. Worlds of fantasy are evoked on Wear your Love like Heaven, The Land Doesn't Have to Be and, perhaps Donovan's quintessential paean to nature and fairytale, Isle of Islay.

Fantasy develops further with Tyrannosaurus Rex's Unicorn (1969) and, particularly, with the publication of Bolan's book, The Warlock of Love (1969), dedicated to the 'woods of knowledge' bearing the influence of W.B.Yeats. The record sleeve of Unicorn shows Bolan and Steve Peregrin Took gazing over a copy of Blake's complete works. (It is interesting to note that there are photos of Nick Drake taken with a volume of Blake's Complete Works as a prop). Sinfield recalls the period: 'It appears we (Sinfield and his first wife, Stephanie Ruben) were sat, late one night, in the restaurant of the infamous Speakeasy, chatting to my late friend Marc Bolan...we were joined by his lovely, witty and wise wife June...it was always a pleasure to talk with the "bopping elf" as he was, at the time, one of the very few people with whom I could discuss and delve into matters of a magical and esoteric nature. During the conversation someone mentioned I must meet...Richard Gardner...leading to a meeting with the painter of the images (on the record sleeve of In the Wake of Poseidon) Tammo (de Jongh).' (69) Sinfield denies any direct influence from Bolan's music and influence, but he was well disposed to introduce the fashionable, the mysterious and the magical into the context of King Crimson. Perhaps it is his unconscious side, in particular, which initiates the presence of the archetype that was referred to as the band's 'good fairy', an invisible presence that the members held responsible for their meteoric rise to prominence? Robert Fripp has said, 'There was something completely other which surrounded this group. I don't believe that we went from abject failure to global musical and commercial success in nine months without something outside the band giving us help. We sometimes mentioned the "good fairy" and had the impression for a time that we could do no wrong, that something special was going on. And it was. At some shows I had extra sensory experiences - of the audience, what was happening or what was about to happen, who had walked into the club, who was listening - that I have never had since...this founding Crimson was charmed... .' (70)

Sinfield has recently spoken about his experience of KC I in relation to the lyrics: 'King Crimson was part of the late '60's counter-cultural *zeitgeist*. The term 'observation' was a subtext that I insisted on from an intellectual point of view.... to come to ITCOTCK...Schizoid Man was a direct result of the Vietnam War. There's a recent book...Four Presidents Lie, or something like that, and the idea is parallel to Schizoid Man: you can't get to be a politician unless you lie. It's a little like the American Indians who were wiped out with smallpox-infected blankets. I Talk to the Wind is like Blowing in the Wind...very simple and concise. It's simply a conversation between a straight man and someone from the counter-cultural generation.' (71) Ian McDonald has said, 'It was a conversation between Pete and a suit (his boss). In fact, I think that I came up with the idea for the lyrics of the chorus.' (72) Sinfield: 'Epitaph is the confusion sown by religious ideologies and had a huge influence on Greg (Lake). Moonchild is about lost innocence and trying to re-live it. I was probably, unconsciously, looking for my mother. Also the striking impression of Stephanie (Ruben) in a black velvet dress when I first knew her. The kind of clothes you could buy at Kensington Market. The Court of the Crimson King is an observation about "spin". No one ever tells the truth. We've been lied to by kings, princes and popes who wish to keep their power. Poets see it from the Machiavellian point of view and see the poor and widows who are the ones who ultimately suffer. That's the way it is. You never hear good things - only things about rapists and murderers. Some people write down what they see.' (73)

Sinfield's vision is an allegory - an observation - listing opposite modes of reality and experience in the culture of the 1960's. In this way it is, perhaps, rather like a modern Songs of Innocence and Experience, sometimes in the style of the period (I Talk to the Wind), sometimes in a neo-Medieval/early Renaissance guise/Gothic-like style (The Court of the Crimson King), imagery that propels it both backwards and forwards by bending the temporal dimension. Indeed, there may be a faint echo of the cynicism found on Frank Zappa's We're Only In It for the Money, as well as some of the material found on The Cheerful Insanity of Giles, Giles and Fripp but completely re-styled. Combined with the many different musical styles, the album reaches across boundaries to a wide and diverse audience in the form of a universal sonic pamphlet which succeeds even more so by the synthesis of musical opposites. With colourful and, sometimes, graphic imagery it may be interpreted polysemantically, as Jon Green has discussed. (74)

Sinfield is quite systematic in his use of poetic devices, as well as practical considerations when writing lyrics. I would like to quote extensively from a lecture given by him in 1997. (75)

'I think it terribly important that you have an underlying motor that drives you along, be it anger and/or passion or life for the work, as well as a certain talent for understanding words and their reason for being written, and to be written excellently...The souls of words and relationship to each other is terribly important...there sounds are "felt" and not simply "heard"...Edith Sitwell's A Poet's Notebook has been extraordinarily valuable to me, both from my understanding of music and also songs...(there is) a particular chapter on techniques of sound and it's applied to poems...of course, lyrics are not necessarily poems, but they have a poetic nature insofar as people can "feel" the ohs', the aah's, the "t" sounds...Greg Lake used to point out to me while we were writing together that he had to stand out in front of fifty thousand people and make them believe what he was saying...It's also very important for musicians to understand what lyrics are saying... What this means is that it gives the song longevity, a timelessness, and it will become a classic...Everything has to be larger than life , in order to reach the listener...(but) what you have are the noises...the sound of words like crowds, queue, jokes, "c" "c" "c" ...you get this sharp cracking sound, and then it softens again...what is very important...is the feel of these hard sounds...Bob Dylan admits to doing the same - it's like playing games, but the games you play with the noises, the sounds and syllables, and especially the consonants...should keep the listener right there, suspended - it's all in the way these are constructed... second verses can be difficult, so you end to go to "scenery" and "open the curtain" as with a play, and so set the mood, as if to say "this is the real point of the song, in the second verse". Like paintings that have light and contrast, songs are very much in tune with the senses, with vibrations...I would say that I actually almost "smell" the words and the sounds - they become shapes, and it's really very organic...I think that's how it's done, and you must get that involved...you should almost act out the characters.'

Musical Guide to In The Court Of The Crimson King by King Crimson

Sinfield connects with technique, atmosphere and imagery in his lyrics. From the start of ITCOTCK short, almost stuttered syllables, and machine gun-like alliteration is deployed, so as to define the theme of Schizoid Man. This is done to heighten the brutality of war, and the t's and s's are rattled out by hard attacks in short, two-line verses of rhyming couplets using trochaic rhythm followed by a short, one line chorus:

> CaT'S fooT, iron Claw
> Neuro-SurgeonS Scream for more
> AT Paranoia'S PoiSon Door
> TwenTy FirST CenTury SChiZoiD man.

The second verse is even more vivid:

> BlooD raCK BarBed wire
> PolitiCianS Funeral Pyre

Here consonance is perhaps the point where hard consonants surround vowels. The sound of words is all-important in the final song, the rock anthem-like The Court of the Crimson King. The first two lines convey the impression both of the sound of prison chains, followed by a sudden flash of sunlight by positioning of consonants utilising onomatopoeia:

> The ruSTeD CHainS of priSon moonS
> Are SHaTTereD by the Sun

The sound of the piper's articulation of the woodwind instrument he plays is also conveyed:

> The PurPle Piper Plays his tune

The same is also applicable in verse two where Sinfield has suggested the curtains be opened to reveal more vivid imagery. Also, onomatopoeia and alliteration brilliantly convey the rattle of metal against metal:

The Keeper of the city Keys

Clearly, Epitaph is a kind of counter-cultural hymn - one

connected to the later In the Wake of Poseidon - but one that has been turned on its head not to glorify the establishment but, conversely, to tear it down. Sinfield resorts to symbolism to convey the confusion sown by dogmas and creeds.

Moonchild is different. The twilight atmosphere of something approaching the garden lovescene in Crowley's novel Moonchild or Dion Fortune's Moon Magic is evoked by the use of assonance:

> Call her mOONchild
> DAncing in shAllows Of a rIver...
> TAlking tO the trEEs Of the
> CObwEb strAnge
> SlEEping on the stEps Of a fOUntain
> WAving sIlver wAnds to the
> NIght-birds sOng
> WAIting for the sUn On the mOUntain.

The many examples of vowels provide the words with circular or rounded images which are particularly fitting in the context of words like 'moon' and 'sundial'. One also thinks of Stéphane Mallarmé's poetry in connection with Moonchild. More importantly, however, Sinfield's word techniques show him as the counter-cultural successor to Beat poet Jack Kerouac who, in his essay The Beginning of Bop, experimented with text-sound and sound poetry. Interestingly, King Crimson's album Beat (1982) was inspired by the Beat poets (Jack Kerouac, Neal Cassady and Allen Ginsberg) and the lyrics (written by Adrian Belew) echo the verbal rhythms they created.

Symbolism and allegory are central to Sinfield's work and, as I have previously discussed, he has spoken about the words of The Court of the Crimson King as representing political spin. The words of the third verse provides an insight into these techniques:

> The gardener plants an evergreen
> Whilst trampling on a flower.
> I chase the wind of a prism ship
> To taste the sweet and sour
>
> The pattern juggler lifts his hand;
> The orchestra begin.

> As slowly turns the grinding wheel
> In the court of the crimson king.

The 'gardener' might be God - an authority figure at least - who, planting the 'evergreen' - the tree of knowledge - treads on a 'flower': an image of nature, innocence, and freedom and an important counter-cultural symbol. 'Chasing the wind' is suggestive of the invisible and the freedom of nature and spirit, while the 'prism' suggests divided light: perhaps the light which is referred to as a symbol of the divine. Put in the context of 'sweet and sour' the opposites of the Tao are suggested. The pattern juggler may represent an orchestral conductor, as well as a circus entertainer, who provides meaningless gestures which are only recognised as collective codes - the orchestra - while the 'grinding wheel' turns slowly in the king's court - bread, as a symbol of finance, is that which makes the world spin. The yellow jester of verse four is an even more striking symbol. The jester is the one closest to the king drawing back any existing veil of illusion. In a sense, he resembles the modern day cartoonist who satirises the machinery of the political arena. In being disconnected from the climbers on the corporate ladder, the jester observes the movers and shakers of the court (the 'puppets'). Furthermore, the king knows the jester will never displace him. Like the joker in the modern pack of cards, or the trickster of the alchemical opus, the jester is able to transform himself into anything at will. Truths such as these leap out at a listener. Sinfield's lyrics, when combined with epoch shaking music and players who understood his intentions, were a blast into the collective consciousness of the time, banging on the door of the establishment for reform.

The painting, which adorns the inner and outer sleeve of ITCOTCK, is by Barry Godber (b. 1946) a friend of Sinfield's from Chelsea Art College. Sinfield has compared him to 'a sort of Nick Drake figure'. (76) According to Sid Smith, Godber became a regular visitor to the basement rehearsal room and designed a poster for the band, as well as designing Michael Giles' double bass drum heads. (77) His paintings for the album came from listening to recordings of the album, then looking into a mirror and painting what he saw, resulting in a frightening self portrait. As Smith has observed, the inside sleeve offers an 'inner peace and calm counterbalance to the fury of the outer cover.' (78) The sleeve set a precedence for the record sleeve design of King Crimson's subsequent albums, by not always including lettering on the cover. This allowed the sleeve to be hung as a poster. However, its real power is in symbolising the music and lyrics contained within, and serves as a visual signifier of enormous power and intensity. In a sense, Barry Godber's artwork became a potent symbol not just for King Crimson, but for the age in which it was painted. To some extent, this was transformed with the Tantric symbol of 1972's Larks' Tongues In Aspic and, again, on into the 1980's with the John Kyrk/Steve Ball knotwork design for the Discipline album which, in turn, became the logo for Fripp's record label, Discipline Global Mobile.

Part 2.
11. The Minutiae of In the Court of the Crimson King

i) The Making of ITCOTCK

Ian McDonald has many vivid memories of the recording of ITCOTCK. (79) 'The recording took eleven days including the mixing and mastering. It was all done on eight tracks with the drums into stereo on two tracks. Everything else was done on the remaining six tracks. We did different things on some tracks. For example, the sax ends abruptly at the end of the solo in Schizoid Man to make way for Robert's guitar which had to go on immediately afterwards. The sound at the beginning of Schizoid Man was this small wind-blown chamber-organ. I can't remember whether or not we hired it or it was already in the studio. I placed my forearm on the keyboard. It was too much for this little keyboard to take. Twenty or thirty notes were depressed. The instrument was also used for the puppets section of the title-track - the tootie bit at the end. For Moonchild the melody in the guitar at the beginning is the sound of the return of the reverb. The original signal for the guitar was taken out leaving the echo of the signal only which sounded very distant. The Moonchild improvisation was a filler. We didn't want a cover version but all original material. We could have used Get Thy

Bearings. For Moonchild, I didn't have a sight-line to Michael and Robert and the vibes were in a vocal booth. It was heard over the headphones. I could hear them but not see them so we didn't, here, rely on visual cues. Greg isn't on the improvisation. We did twelve hour sessions for the recording. Charlotte (Bates) called me at 10 in the morning when I'd just returned from the studio. I think she was impressed by this. We didn't formulate a musical strategy. We had a go at Lucy In The Sky With Diamonds and Michael From The Mountains just to see where it would lead us. I'd had military band experience. I'd also had ear-training lessons and lessons in orchestration, learnt clarinet and played in a wind quintet and dance band. That's where my Three Score and Four was performed, which became the basis of the Mirrors section of Schizoid Man.' McDonald has also said, (80) ' We were just making a record. We were kids given a studio to play with. There was an incredible energy. Schizoid Man was done in one take on August 1st, 1969. Greg's voice was treated with distortion on the vocal channel. Michael played slightly open hi-hat on every beat of the bar using an equiliser which altered the tone. For the angst-ridden solo in Schizoid Man I put myself in discomfort by adopting uncomfortable playing positions." Peter Sinfield's first wife, Stephanie Ruben, has said that King Crimson Mk I was really Ian's band. (81) Robert Fripp: (82) 'It was the melodic detail I loved so much about Ian. He should have all the credit that's due. "Let There Be Light" from Drivers Eyes was the first time I heard an authentic McDonald/Sinfield song since 1969, and what a song!'

ii) Musical Techniques

In the light of Progressive rock, ITCOTCK resembles a five-movement orchestral song-cycle. In the light of the counter-cultural period from which it derives, it is a sonic pamphlet for that generation, utilising as wide a range of musics as possible yet retaining a remarkable consistency. What's more, it has a maturity unlike so many other musical artefacts from the period which, musically and sonically speaking, have dated. The musics may be labelled: jazz-rock (Schizoid Man); jazz-folk (I Talk to the Wind); counter-cultural hymn (Epitaph); Renaissance-like with a long free-jazz coda (Moonchild); anthem (The Court of the Crimson King).

Texturally, the work incorporates a wide variety of types from the screeching saxes, screaming and distorted guitars and compressed drums of Schizoid Man; the soft and spacious I Talk to the Wind; the mellotron-drenched Epitaph; the fleeting and distant Moonchild and the acoustic guitar and mellotron-led title track. The textures of these are juxtaposed to provide maximum contrast, as well as delineating the structure and shape of the whole. See Diagram 1.

The five-song structure of ITCOTCK was to be adopted for subsequent King Crimson albums, not exactly but in essence. Sub-titles were also included for reasons both poetic and realistic.

Although there may be a similarity to nineteenth century symphonic forms, there is also a passing allusion to the seventeenth and eighteenth century musical forms such as ritornello and obbligato. Baroque-like imagery, included in Sinfield's lyrics, is reflected in the ground-bass of Epitaph: See Example 7.

Baroque structural types also have much in common with the heads (choruses/ritornello) and verses (instrumental solos/episodes/obbligato) of jazz and jazz-rock. This similarity has probably more to do with the call and response archetypes of non-white musics , but in this context it's as though a hybrid has been created which marks the beginnings of the Progressive rock style. However, when I asked Ian McDonald if this was the case he answered that he was thinking more in terms of song structures than jazz.

iii) Song structures

Song structures on ITCOTCK are long (Schizoid Man = 7:23; I Talk to the Wind = 6:05; Epitaph: 8:47; Moonchild: 12:12; ...Court = 9:22), as opposed to the three minute types found in some other popular music contexts. Clearly the intention is to listen rather than dance. There are five songs in all and each of them is exclusively strophic, where different words are repeated to the same music, allowing opportunity for repetition. I will deal with the structure of each song separately.

Schizoid Man (SM) The piece is powered by the strong riff played by the full band. The three sung verses of SM are relatively short, three bars long with a condensed chorus coming in the fourth bar emphasising the words, 'Twenty First Century Schizoid Man.' The middle of the song, subtitled Mirrors, is a long section of guitar and alto sax solos recalling Bebop jazz climaxing on a section of fast unison riffs. Verse three follows four bars of fast rising semitones in the instrumental parts. The song itself is framed by two sections of noise: at the beginning played as clustered pitches on chamber pipe organ; at the end, a loud free-form improvisation. See Diagram 2.

I Talk to the Wind (ITTTW) Moving to the polar opposite from SM, ITTTW is similar structurally but texturally reduced except it includes a longer chorus. It has two flute parts, two clarinet parts, two vocal parts and solo flute and guitar solos. Structurally, ITCOTCK rests on its use of contrast. See Diagram 3.

Epitaph Epitaph is segued from ITTTW, first with a fade followed by a huge timpani crescendo into the song itself, balanced in the centre of the song by a rising diminished chord on C. It is hymn-like in its dimensions. See Diagram 4. Epitaph is harmonically unresolved at the end. The song is hymn-like, something consciously conceived by Peter Sinfield. (83) The introductory sections to each verse are felt to be be ritornello-like per se, with the memorable bent upwards/downwards guitar lines.

Moonchild The order of verse and chorus is switched here but are joined, and two-thirds of the song is a long free-form instrumental. See Diagram 5.

The Court of the Crimson King The title track is anthemic in structure and delivery with chorus fused to verse. The latter mellotron ritornelli (refrains) are expanded in terms of their repetitions. See Diagram 6.

iv) Melodic Motif

The vocal lines throughout ITCOTCK are connected by melodic

motifs: usually a descending Minor or Major third: See Example 8 (SM), Example 9 (ITTTW), Example 10 (Epitaph), Example 11 (Moonchild) and Example 12 (TCOTCK).

These, combined with the harmony, give the music a sense of melancholy. Almost exclusively, vocal phrases tend to fall towards the end of lines. With the exception of SM which rises to the condensed chorus, 'Twenty First Century Schizoid Man' and TCOTCK, which does a similar thing. Whether the composers did this intentionally or not is difficult to say but the important point to make is the words and music conjure-up an imaginary landscape both of the (then) contemporary landscape, and a feeling of something other: a mythical landscape which could, perhaps, be called a glimpse of the collective unconscious. Mythical subjects were used more or less exclusively in Baroque opera.

Included alongside the third motif is a half-step (Minor second or semitone) which appears in different guises: sometimes as melodic inflection, sometimes as part of the vocal line and sometimes in the instrumental lines. Metaphorically, it may be thought of as 'anguished', reinforcing the melancholic character of the third, and when combined with it in a vocal phrase produces an extremely potent effect: See Example 13 (SM) and Example 14 (ITTTW).

Interestingly, in ITTTW it is used as part of a falling chromatic line in the inside part (tenor of the piano part) culminating in an E - D~ suspension: See Example 15 (ITTTW) and Example 16 (Epitaph),

In Epitaph (Greg Lake was responsible for writing the melody over Ian McDonald's mellotron chords: E minor second inversion [Eminor/B], D major second inversion [D/A], A minor seventh, B aug - B major) (84), the falling half-step is taken into the larger-scale harmonic scheme of the coda: C Major seventh - B Minor as well as the end of the choruses (see Chorus 1, 2:02ff and coda, 6: 57ff) underpinning the word 'crying'. In this case there's a connection with Henry Purcell's Dido's Lament from his opera, Dido and Aeneas (1689). See Example 17 (Moonchild) and Example 18 (TCOTCK).

Most of the half-steps tend to fall at the beginning or end of phrases, such as the E - D# suspension in ITTTW (in the vocal parts), which means that harmonic resolution or a melodic movement upwards is the only way out of the conflict. Indeed, the lack of resolution is the whole idea behind Epitaph as Ian McDonald has mentioned. (85)

v) Melodic motifs in the instrumental parts

The instrumental phrasing in SM mainly ascends to balance with the descending phrases in the vocal part. Here, the semitones rise as part of the hard riff of the ritornello: See Example 19. The addition of rising semitones to Greg Lake's original six-note riff was Ian McDonald's idea. (86) It connects to the rising semitone in the guitar part of TCOTCK (see Ex. 36). The Minor/Major third and ½-step are included together in a chain and reflected by inversion in the section called Mirrors: See Examples 20a and 20b. The guitar solo extends the ½-step in the Dorian mode (transposed to C Minor) which makes the second and third and sixth and seventh degrees of the scale ½-steps: See Example 21. Or sometimes with the addition of F# makes the scale partly symmetrical if the G natural is removed: See Example 22. Fripp's penchant for octatonic and whole-tone harmony is, of course, used to great effect in the output of King Crimson Mk III as well as his more recent work (see Andrew Keeling - Musical Guide to Larks' Tongues in Aspic - Spaceward Graphics). The ½-steps in the guitar solo are found in places: See Example 23. Ian McDonald: 'Robert Fripp didn't listen to Chuck Berry, therefore his guitar playing was original." (87) The climax of the Minor third/½-step motif is found in the unison riff which McDonald says was written in 8/8: See Example 24. The bass guitar part during the instrumental solo is like a chromatic or walking bass. Found in jazz, it is full of ½-step runs as well as transforming the Mirrors riff (see Ex. 20) into full steps (Major second's) alongside the original Minor third: See Example 25,

ITTTW features both Minor thirds and ½-steps in the flute duet at the beginning of the song. The suspension (E-D#) may also be found in other contexts: See Example 26. The guitar solo also has a chain of ½ steps: See Example 27. The final flute solo includes chains of the interval: See Example 28.

Epitaph is notable for the ½-step in the guitar part picked-up, in part, from the same at 3:32 of ITTTW. It also includes the Minor third: See Example 29. The A Minor9th chord, in the acoustic guitar part at 1:32, takes the ½-step into the wider harmonic context: here, there is an allusion to J.S. Bach's Prelude in C Major. See Example 30. It's also found in the clarinet solo at 5:01ff, which is kicked-off by the Minor third: See Example 31.

Moonchild includes a descending ½-step (semitone) line, connecting to the piano accompaniment in ITTTW, as well as with the ascending/descending B, C, C# in the guitar part of TCOTCK (see Ex. 36): See Example 32. The mellotron part also includes it: See Example 33. The long instrumental improvisation utilises the motif to great effect both as a melodic and harmonic interval. The summation of both motifs is found in the title-track, initially in the opening mellotron ritornello: See Example 34. The ½-step ascent at 0:11 was taken from Sam and Dave. (88) Rising semitones are also found in the flute solo and, particularly, in the guitar counter-melody (4:14ff) which connects to the G-F# ½-step of Epitaph. Indeed, the guitar part is notable for the upward/downward semitones which also, in turn, connect to the same in Mirrors of SM: See Example 35. More importantly, it is a transformation of the basic E Minor9th chord found in the introduction to verse 4 of the title-track: See Example 36. This includes the rising and falling half-steps respectively: B-C, C#-C natural (pitch classes: 7-8, 9-8) also found in Fripp's transformation of it (see Ex. 35). Robert Fripp says: 'The guitar part is my main contribution. Ian showed me the E Minor9th (found in verse 4) which I took as a beginning point and kept going!' (89) McDonald says that Fripp adapted it to the harmonics found as the accompaniment in verse 1 of the song. (90) The ½-step is taken into the wider harmonic context in the mellotron ritornello connecting it to the coda of Epitaph and the suspensions in ITTTW.

The pitches in John Barry's James Bond theme are: See Example 37. Interestingly, the 'swing' section of the Bond theme also has some relation to the main theme of Pictures of a City, written as A Man, A City, and performed by King Crimson Mk I: See Example 38. Perhaps these are, after all, allusions to the urban, the contemporary world of the 1960's which was eyed suspiciously by the counter-culture and seen as being part of the consumer-driven mass culture. These allusions occur in songs one, three and five on ITCOTCK which are centred on war, religion and politics respectively. Certainly, Pictures of a City is a graphic portrayal of New York City.

It's worth concluding that the music on this album seems not to rely on bolt-on structures, as compared to the music of some of its contemporaries, but is of an organic nature, where intervals are not just projected forwards and backwards during the work, but are subjected to transformation and growth and, ultimately, taken into the wider-scale structural context. It's difficult to say which came first, chicken or egg. However, this makes the structure coherent and on a par with similar kinds of compositional procedures found in the classical music sonata form tradition.

vi) Harmony (1)

The harmony (and chords) used on the album have structural implications for the work as a whole. The 'affect' produced by each key/mode, combined with the motif, texture, orchestration and dynamics, determines the psychological impact the music has on a listener. Certainly, this is true of all music, but with ITCOTCK it is decisive. When combined with Sinfield's lyrics it is optimal. The key of each may be seen in the following scheme: See Diagram 7.

Vocal and instrumental ranges are also important for the success of a song. For example, there are several recorded versions of ITTTW, but three notable ones: a) Giles, Giles and Fripp/early KC-period; b) BBC radio broadcast; c) definitive ITCOTCK version. Featuring Judy Dyble on vocals, version a) is cast in A Major largely to suit the range of female vocals. Version c) is in E Major which is more in keeping with Greg Lake's vocal range, but is also more successful in the definitive version with the upward modulation from the C Minor of Schizoid Man which precedes it. E major is also a more expansive and resonant key bearing in mind the range of the flute. ITTTW, when it finally arrives, is even more surprising than it may otherwise have been had it been in A Major. The E Major of the song also makes for a fluid transition to the dark E Minor mode of Epitaph. Modes are adopted throughout with occasional references to keys. See Diagram 8. This might be pushed further to include the positive and negative views as adopted by the counter-culture to the establishment. See Diagram 9

ITCOTCK, as its subtitle implies, observes the cultural landscape of the 1960's, whereas the second album, In the Wake of Poseidon, continues the theme set by the first, but also offers an alternative as documented by Tammo de Jongh and Richard Gardner (see Andrew Keeling - Musical Guide to In the Wake of Poseidon). King Crimson's third album, Lizard, develops the theme further, with the stylistic model from ITCOTCK, as well as the structural types, being carried-over to these later records. When the shift to a new and different focus in the music of King Crimson happened from 1972 onwards - yet retaining important elements of the early King Crimson - it was to correspond with the death-throes of counter-cultural thought. These kind of paradigm shifts have occurred throughout King Crimson history.

vii) Harmony (2)

I have previously discussed the ½-step motif at the back of the album. The E Minor9 chord sequence at 5:42 of the title-track (see Ex. 36) is a fingerprint that became closely identified with King Crimson. It reappears, for example, in the coda of Exiles from Larks' Tongues in Aspic. Exotic chords are found throughout the music of King Crimson, such as the mellotron anacrusis to Lizard, which also uses the ½-step concept although, this time, there are three interpretations of labelling: a) Dominant 13th in close position (in A modal Minor); b) an F Minor chord superimposed on an E7 chord; c) adjacent semitones: See Example 39. This kind of chord is a worthy successor to the Minor 9th archetype found in the work under discussion, and a bridge to the octatonic and whole-tone aggregates found respectively in Larks' Tongues in Aspic and Red.

I wonder if John Barry's theme from the Bond movies of the 1960's, as the rising ½-step B-C-C#-C, has an unconscious influence on the voice-leading of the Minor 9th chord sequence found in ITCOTCK. Peter Sinfield: 'These things operate unconsciously. You went into a cinema and came out singing something you'd heard. Jon Anderson was influenced by the theme from Bonanza, for example. These things must affect us.' (91) In turn, the 007 theme owes something to the early instrumentals by The Shadows, particularly Apache (1960), Man of Mystery (1960/61) and FBI (1961)

I will refer to each song in turn, with particular attention to the Minor 9th archetype as well as other features in the harmonic field of ITCOTCK.

Schizoid Man - I have already commented on the rising ½-steps as motif in the parallel power chords of the SM riff. They appear again three octaves higher in the high guitar/alto sax bends, where the 2nd string is bent to first string, a la Hendrix, and alto sax pitches are lip-bent: See Example 40.

SM is, essentially, a riff-based song and the ½-steps permeate its fabric. The song is centred on C Minor Dorian and the key is used more or less exclusively, except for the semitone power chords which rise F(IV) - F#(#IV) - G(V) and occasional shifts to V (G Minor/Bb) in the short chorus at 4:35 or to prepare the manic unison/stop-start riffs at 4:40 which begin as an elaboration on V (G). The purpose of this G (V) prolongation in the 'stop-start' section is to wind-up the tension to breaking-point. These riffs do eventually return to C Minor, but the C Minor, here, is no longer felt as the home key. G has now taken on the role of the tonic (I). It's as though the longer a key is hammered home, the more imprinted it becomes on the mind as key-centre. C Minor is, however, re-established as the tonic (I) at 5:25 with the Mirrors riff. The chromaticism of SM (in particular the rising ½-steps connected at ground level connected to the chordal archetype) finally anticipates the coda with a written-out accelerando: See Example 41.

The chromaticism can only be pushed one stage further: into the aleatoric, free-form blow at 6:56. It's though it's the only place the music can go, recalling the method used by Arvo Part in his choral work, Credo. The striking thing about SM is its jazz-like feel, differentiating the music of King Crimson from other Progressive rock bands, with the walking/chromatic bass lines, drumming and sax and guitar solos. Here, the influence of John Handy's Spanish Lady, from the 'Live at the Monterey Jazz Festival' (1965), stands out. Yet SM is high-powered jazz rock - certainly not in a Handy or, even, a Weather Report style - with a hard rock edge, yet even this is rounded out by Fripp's guitar chords which are minor, proper: See Example 42.

The hard-edge is provided by the first bass part (i.e. there are two bass guitar parts: one fuzzed; one clean) which follows the melody of the sax part two octaves lower. Ian McDonald's big band piece Three Score and Four, written a number of years prior to SM, is the basis for the Mirrors section: See Example 43.

ITTTW - The richness and beauty of ITTTW owes much to its E Major/Mixolydian key. The shift from E major to C major7 to G major7 to F# minor and finally cadencing on B major. See Example 44.

The chorus includes oscillating chords of E Major and B Minor (note the absence of Dominant sevenths).

Epitaph - The song includes the first complete example of the E Minor9 archetype in the acoustic guitar part (0:04) (see Ex. 36) as an A Minor9 (0:11). The pathos induced by the Minor 9ths is one of the enduring fingerprints of ITCOTCK. The descending and repeated chord progression E Minor - D Major - A Minor7 - B aug -B major (6-5 suspension) is a ground-bass which influenced subsequent bands who referred to themselves as Progressive. Variants are found in The Pretty Things' I See You, ELP's Stones of Years (part of the Tarkus suite) and Barclay James Harvest's song Mockingbird. The introduction and verse are underpinned solely by the ground further relating ITCOTCK to Baroque musical models. The chorus is essentially an oscillation between two chords: E Minor and B Minor, with the chorus end concentrating on the C Major - B Minor Phrygian descent, heightening the tension through three repetitions. Indeed, the tension between the D# of the B Major and the D Natural of the B Minor is another factor underlining the song's innate conflict which, together with the ½-step G-F# in the guitar's chordal E Minor9, creates an apt soundscape for Lake's dramatic delivery of Sinfield's terrifying vision of the contemporary politico-religious establishment. The coda's C Major - B Minor repetitions winds-up the unresolved lyrics to an even greater degree. The C Major - B Minor shift reappears in Lizard, underpinning the alto sax solo in Cirkus. It also appears as a true Phrygian (F Major7b5 - E Minor) in Forever and Ever on Ian McDonald's album, Drivers Eyes (1999). The Phrygian harmonic shift is also the basis of Renaissance's Kings and Queens included on their eponymous album (1969).

Moonchild - The song is in the Aeolian mode except for the descending ½-step line made of chromatic pitches (see Ex. 32). In some ways the song is like a short-phrased Pavane. The pitches of the verse includes the following pentatonic scale: See Example 45. The chorus uses the entire Aeolian aggregate minus the sixth: See Example 46.

The feeling is at once early Renaissance-like with it's gentle bass-absent texture. The ad lib. improvisation includes many examples of dissonant harmony, but its success lies in the fact that the pitches are mostly culled from the home mode centering a listener, and the music invariably returns to the mode centre. The shimmering vibes emerge from the decaying guitar at 2:22, and the pitches are all Aeolian. Here, the guitar plays, from time to time, A Minor/F root (F Major seventh) and C Major seventh last inversion, a chord made from the pitches of the home mode: See Example 47.

The chordal archetype is also used, but this time spelt as A Minor sixth and A Minor ninth: See Example 48. Alternating between modes using the same pitches (i.e. A Minor mode, C Major, Lydian) is something Robert Fripp has taken as his own, cropping-up in Guitar Craft instruction techniques. The texture becomes linear from 3:51ff with the entry of the gentle cymbals and the development of the ½-step motif with an E root: See Example 49. The jazz-like arabesque in the clean, bass-toned guitar is also all white note: See Example 50. This cadences on the dominant with ½-step trills giving the music a Spanish effect: See Example 51. Signalling a change of mood with the arrival of muted percussion, woods and rim-shots, the ½-step widens to a tone at 4:50: See Example 52. With the ½-step returning at 4:55: See Example 53. In a combination of a trill with a two-note oscillation, the guitar cadences from the ½-step: See Example 54.

Musical Guide to In The Court Of The Crimson King by King Crimson

A texture of rapid scales emerges at 5:33, creating a humorous dialogue between all three players. Here, short attacks in the guitar are often sustained in the vibraphone, with short bursts in the percussion on skin, metal and wood. Following a cadence at 8:54 comes a section of near-quotations: the classical guitar piece Malaguena at 9:04, in A Minor, touches on the dominant; Surrey with a Fringe on Top at 9:49, from the musical Oklahoma. Quotations were a feature that Fripp and Sinfield went on to explore in the Devil's Triangle (Mars) on the subsequent In the Wake of Poseidon. Quotes were also used in King Crimson Mk I 'live' performance. A gong-like cymbal signals a return to the home key and the arrival of sleigh-bells marks the tranquil A major coda, with bass drum and sleigh-bells marking the beat at 11:45 underpinning the delicate vibraphone with its repeated chiming C# and A. Moonchild provides welcome release from the tension of the preceding Epitaph. The improvisation owes something to the Derek Bailey/Gavin Bryars/Tony Oxley trio, Joseph Holbrooke, and the John Stevens/Derek Bailey-led Spontaneous Music Ensemble particularly Sequence I found on the album Withdrawal (1967). Jamie Muir, who later joined the Larks' Tongues in Aspic-period King Crimson, had played alongside Gavin Bryars, Derek Bailey and John Stevens in the Music Improvisation Society.

TCOTCK - The initial mellotron-drenched ritornello is interesting for the following reasons. First, the line includes three chords; it is a sequence, per se; it includes a chain of suspensions. Apropos Example 55: the song begins on a D Major chord [a] with the F# suspended over into the following C Major chord [b] making the F# both a tritone from [c], and rise upwards to the G of the C Major chord [d] then downwards to an E. Here, it resembles a conventional eschappée. The F#/C tritone, and its subsequent resolution, also refers to the 'sweet and sour' found in the lyrics of verse three. The E Natural, of the C Major chord, is suspended over into the major chord, rising to an F# [e] and then downwards to D# of the B major chord. A partially chromatic line rises from B to E# (F natural) [g] (note the tritone) before resolving to the F# of the D Major chord and a repetition of the line. The second time around, the music comes to rest on a B. B is the dominant (V) of E Minor, the key of the song proper, which makes sense of the ritornello. In the context of E Minor, D Major is the lowered leading-note (VII) (in E Minor Aeolian it is VII, per se); C Major is the submediant (VI); B Major, the dominant (V). See Example 55. Beyond this, it demonstrates another descending line as I have previously revealed: See Example 56.

This descending ritornello leads the ear, in dramatic fashion, into Fripp's transformation of McDonald's E Minor ninth chord sequence (see Ex. 35). During the verse, besides the E Minor ninth, chords of A Minor ninth and A Minor sixth/ninth are used as a lute-like accompaniment. Drums provide the anacrustic thrust back into the ritornello. The middle mellotron solo, known as The Return of the Fire Witch (2:20ff) is notable for its alternating D-C chords, elaborated as D/D9 - C - D6 in the organ accompaniment: See Example 57. It is, in fact, simply an elaboration of the ritornello. The flute solo, at 4:14, slims-down the texture to bass guitar and cymbals accompaniment, adding guitar at 4:42, making the ritornello early-Renaissance broken consort-like. The swelling of the mellotron-dominated texture leads to a B Major (V) at 5:17, and then into the E Minor9th chord at 5:24. Here, it is as though the B-C natural-C#-C natural semitones in the acoustic guitar are felt as the climax and logical extension of the rising/descending 1/2-step motif featured throughout the album. Although the rising semitones have appeared throughout the song, as part of the A Minor 9th chord at 0:44 for example, it is only from 5:24ff that the chordal archetype appears in its prime form, together with the rising and falling semitone voice-leading. The bright orchestration of trilling flute, mellotron and rolled cymbals heighten both the 1/2-step voice-leading in the acoustic guitar part, but also point-up the key of E minor which, following the Schenkerian graphs (see Exs. 58 - 60), is the tonic key of the whole work. The rising semitones also create a link with those found in the riffs of SM, producing architectural circularity as well as musical unity. This is felt as a point of arrival, especially as the ½-step - this time F Natural to E Natural - sounding in the electric guitar at 5:40, paints the words 'The yellow jester does not play/But gently pulls the strings' just before the return of the ritornello. Dance of the Puppets is a further elaboration of the ritornello (7:17), this time humorous, performed by McDonald and Giles on pipe-organ. (92) Here, this modified ritornello is in E major picking-up from the tierce de picardie which has brought the music to a partial climax at 6:42. It appears in soft staccato chords, underpinning the melody on the off-beats. The accompaniment is stretched to tied-notes over the barline from 7:43 ff. The final ritornello is performed six times loudly, with additions of (loud) mellotron on accordion setting (left and right in the stereo) and Hammond organ glissandi with a fierce point of arrival at 9:15 for the final chord sustained over two bars, with a final glissando on the final beat of the second bar at 9:21 which completes the song and the entire work.

To summarise, songs 1, 3 and 5 are related by subject-matter: 1 (SM) = war; Epitaph = politico-religious; 5 (TCOTCK) = spin/greed. TCOTCK ends a Major third higher than the opening SM. Songs 2 and 4 are related by fifths: See Diagram 10. As I have previously suggested, in terms of harmonic and intervallic content, the music on the album is not relying on bolt-on structures (as is found in some other Progressive rock works), but is organic: intervals of thirds and seconds (½-steps) are projected forward and backwards throughout, binding each song together with the potential for transformation and growth. Although I am reluctant to use graphic analyses, it does seem that the ½-step is felt as an elaboration in the middle ground of the entire work: See Example 58

I hesitate to offer an Ersatz (a background graph), but let it be said that classical Schenkerian approaches illustrate a descent based on Species Counterpoint such as: See Example 59. However, I can't help thinking that ITCOTCK doesn't recognise traditional schemes but, rather, adapts them (which is a feature of Progressive rock approaches to classical structures) here illustrating a descent in parallel fifths, fitting for a rock music opus: See Example 60. Put simply, Schenkerian analysis is a school of thought pioneered by the German composer/theorist Heinrich Schenker (1868-1935) aimed at revealing the architectural background in a piece of music, through the gradual reduction of surface elaboration. Personally, I have found it useful when applied to rock music pieces (either songs, instrumentals or entire works). Classical Schenkerians may well frown at this suggestion but, following my introductory statements regarding the adaptation of analytical techniques, this is what leaps out of the music.

Rhythm

Many of the metres in ITCOTCK are in 4/4, although there are examples of 12/8, as in Schizoid Man. The high rhythmic energy of SM is appropriate for the album's opener and the pulse of Mirrors remains, more or less, consistent with the pulse of the ritornello and verse/chorus even though it changes to 12/8. There is a difference in tempo between the two, but not massively substantial. The feel of the crotchets is mirrored by dotted crotchets as: a) ritornello/verse/chorus = crotchet 69 (4/4); b) Mirrors = dotted-crotchet 80 (12/8). (As a comparison, the David Cross Band's version of Schizoid Man has the ritornello/verse/chorus at crotchet 66, but Mirrors remains in 4/4 but at crotchet 132 rather than the 12/8 of the original King Crimson version. [See Alive in the Underworld - Noisy Records, 2008]).

Schizoid Man is, of course, differentiated from the other pieces by its intense rhythmic energy, powered by the rhythm section of Greg Lake and Michael Giles, who operate as a jazz team. Giles' drumming, just before the outset of verse 1 demonstrates his striking use of the snare together with the kick-drum: See Example 61. The bass and drums are the engine which drive the music forward demonstrating the close pairing of the rhythm section, and Giles' technique of placing snare on beat one of a bar and playing every beat of the bar on the kick-drum: See Example 62.

I personally remember a review of the McDonald and Giles album (Island Records, 1970) which suggested that a listener should play the record through at least once solely for the drumming alone. This is no less true for ITCOTCK. During the guitar solo of SM there are examples of Giles playing semi-quavers (double - footwork) with the kick-drum, driving the music even more, and filling-in any gaps left by the relatively empty soloistic texture. The section of 'stop-start' unison riffs is played on snare alone, marking the whole band in a tight rhythmic unison: See Example 63. The free-form coda is a section of senza-misura. I have previously suggested that this is the only place in which the pitch can go, and the same applies to the rhythm.

ITTTW serves as a brake to the intensity of SM's rhythmic drive.

It is marked at crotchet 80, and sticks consistently to that throughout. Here, the long harmonic rhythms give the music a chance to breathe; the listener opportunity to reflect. During the verse, in terms of the percussion, soft cymbals are used mostly to mark the off-beats. The crotchet triplets in the flute part, subsequently taken up by the voice, add to the sense of rhythmic arrest. During the chorus, drums play a reasonably standard rock rhythm, although offset by the complexity in the kick-drum part. At 0:56 the imaginative drumming keeps the music moving forward: See Example 64. It's these points of interest that give the music rhythmic impetus. The arabesques in Ian McDonald's central virtuoso flute solo are jazz-like with syncopations and arpeggios: See Example 65.

Epitaph is the slowest piece (Crotchet = 63), positioned in the centre of the structure. In 4/4, this symphonic movement's point of arrival has been anticipated throughout. It seems completely right when it finally arrives. Again, the harmonic rhythm is slow - as expected from a ground-bass - with one chord per bar, speeding-up to two at the cadence (E minor second inversion [E minor/B], D major second inversion [D/A], A minor7, B aug - B major). The textural pause (0:35), at the end of the symphonic ritornello, anticipates the sung verse perfectly. All interest is on the voice, accompanied only by the ground-bass (in the bass guitar) and drums. Triplets are at the centre of the vocal rhythm: See Example 66. The feel is funereal, the drums providing the march-like rhythm. There is no ride-cymbal, just snare and kick-drum: See Example 67. At 1:09 the acoustic guitar plays the downbeat, gradually picking-up with semi-quavers at 1:21, recalling the classical guitar Etudes of Carulli and Carcassi. This gives the music some sense of movement. The chorus is the point at which things become more rhythmically disparate with organ and bass playing together, and guitar and drums playing together: See Example 68. Clearly this is not standard rock texturing. Only later in the verse and on into verse two does the rhythm gain a fluency more usually associated with rock, with the drums picking-up a similar rhythm as found in the previous ITTTW, only here played with greater intensity. There's also a sense that ITTTW and Epitaph are parts of a joined structure which is partly true with the cross-fade coming between them. The central March for No Reason is ponderous with the dark, octave clarinet texture mainly in semi-breves, gradually turning into crotchets with the transformation of the vocal melody.

Acoustic guitar and drums are, this time around, separated in time: See Example 69. The coda is felt as the rhythmic climax of the song, with the foregrounded quaver triplets in the first mellotron part suspended over the barline: See Example 70. The drums are notable for the sheer scope of Giles' technique, especially the rolls at the end of bars, with timpani rolls coming on alternate bars. This always provides the slow harmonic rhythm with a feeling of movement and with points of arrival.

Moonchild is in 4/4 and its metronome speed matches that of ITTTW (i.e. crotchet - 80 c.). This makes for a, more or less, symmetrical rhythmic structure of the songs (i.e. - SM - Crotchet = 69 and middle section - dotted crotchet = 80; ITTTW - crotchet = 80; Epitaph - crotchet = 63; Moonchild - crotchet = 80; TCOTCK - crotchet = 72). The rhythm guitar accompaniment provides the rhythmic momentum through the use of the descending Pavane-like, chromatic ground-bass (see Ex. 32) of two quavers followed by a crotchet and so on. The percussion is used mainly for decoration (i.e. bells of cymbals), allowing the long notes of the high guitar part and the vocals in the chorus, to resonate clearly. Muted drums are included in the verse and provide a sense of movement: See Example 71

The improvisation (The Dream and The Illusion) is initially static and performed ad. lib (it is, after all, an improvisation) which nods not just at the free-form world of jazz, but at contemporary classical works such as Berio's chamber piece Circles and Boulez's Le Marteau sans Maitre. Passages of completely free-form playing are followed by pulse-orientated passages such as at 4:10ff, where a 4/4 metre develops, or at 4:31 where the guitar plays in a recognisable 7/8 metre. This, along with the return to the song's A (Aeolian) centre, accounts for the success of Moonchild. The places of instrumental dialogue are clearly played senza-misura, capturing the dream and illusory quality in the lyrics. The song/improvisation allows for a definite point of respite before the dramatic and anthemic title-track. Fripp: 'Moonchild: the music was completely written by myself, other than Ian McDonald changing two notes, to the immense benefit of the melody (the F at the end of a line which resolves to E [i.e. the ½-step - see the previous section on Motif. A.K.]). The guitar line was laid down as a guide track, but kept.' (93) Ian McDonald: 'Even though the improvisation was just a filler, on listening it seems to get better with time. I'm glad it finishes in a major key (thanks to Robert) which ties in with Peter's last line: sun child. I also remember coming up with the chords for the verse: the A minor root, C major7 second inversion, F# minor half-diminished and F minor with a raised seventh sequence'. (94)

TCOTCK's triumphant arrival is introduced by a five semi-quaver drum anacrusis into the blazing D Major opening of the ritornello. The five semiquaver drum anacrusis is also foreshadowed in ITTTW at 4:47 leading into the flute solo. (Five is regarded, in occult terms, as a magical number. See: Andrew Keeling - Musical Guide to Larks' Tongues in Aspic). Rhythmically, the song is in 4/4 and is reasonably four-square, marked at crotchet = 72. This makes it memorable, especially the ritornello with its choral-like harmony vocals. The only section where the music is rhythmically embellished is in the vocal part and during the middle flute solo (4:14) with the contrapuntal interplay of the guitar part. The acoustic guitar creates forward motion with the E Minor9th chord at 5:24. The bass pitches of the chamber organ ritornello, Dance of the Puppets, are tied across bar-lines derailing the four-squareness and creating a sense of counterpoint: See Example 72.

The silence that precedes Dance of the Puppets creates expectation, functioning as an anacrusis to the final ritornello. There are many sonic embellishments to this deep inside the texture such as organ syncopations and glissandi, giving the music a sense of instability and chaos. Fripp: 'I believe that the reprise/theme/recapitulation/coda in TCOTCK was my suggestion. This also suggests that the overall form was a primary concern.' (95).

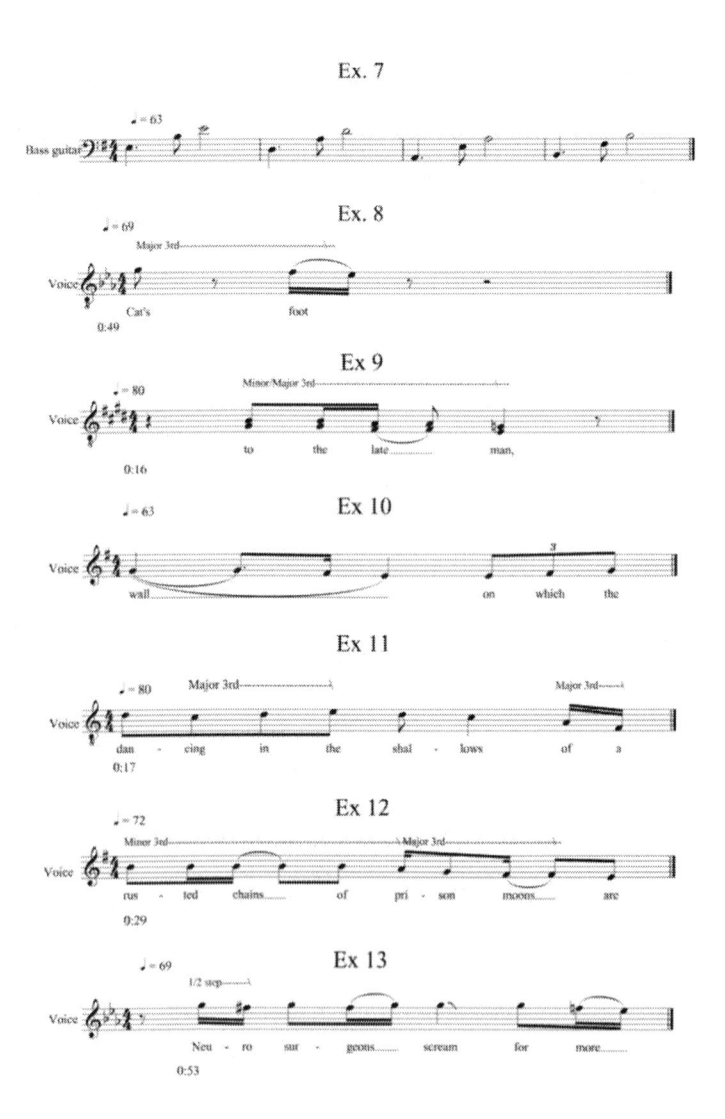

Musical Guide to In The Court Of The Crimson King by King Crimson

Ex. 7

Ex. 8

Ex 9

Ex 10

Ex 11

Ex 12

Ex 13

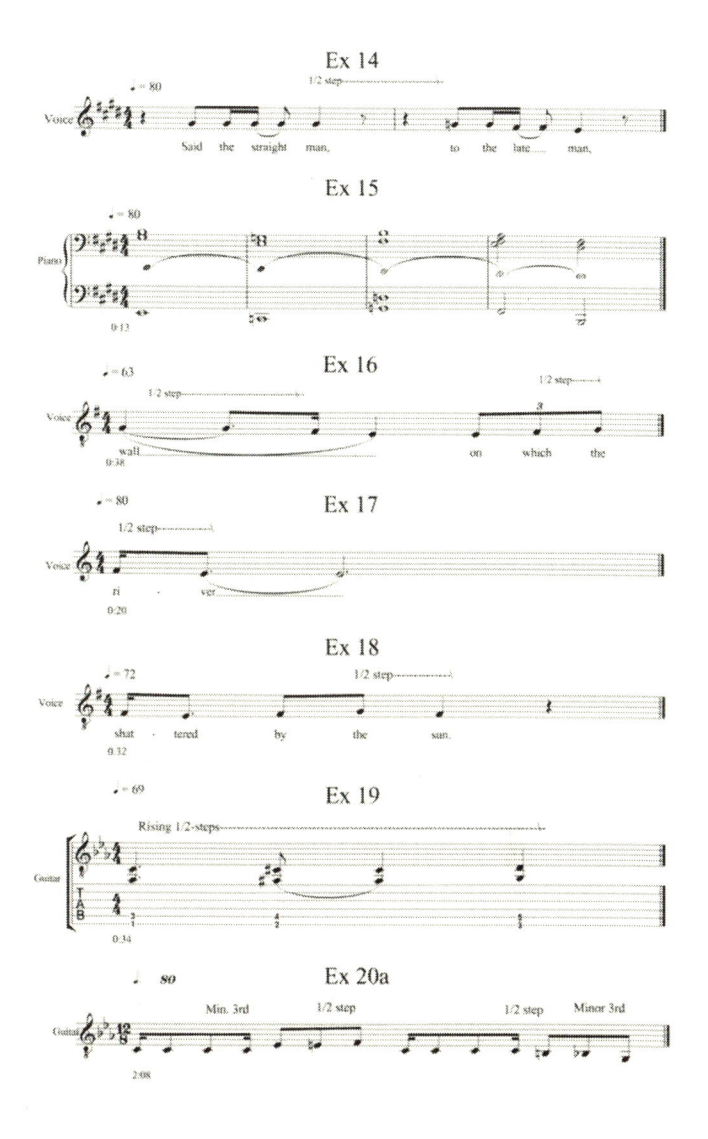

Musical Guide to In The Court Of The Crimson King by King Crimson

Musical Guide to In The Court Of The Crimson King by King Crimson

Ex 20b

Ex 21

Ex 22

Ex 23

Ex 24

Ex 25

Ex 26

Ex 27

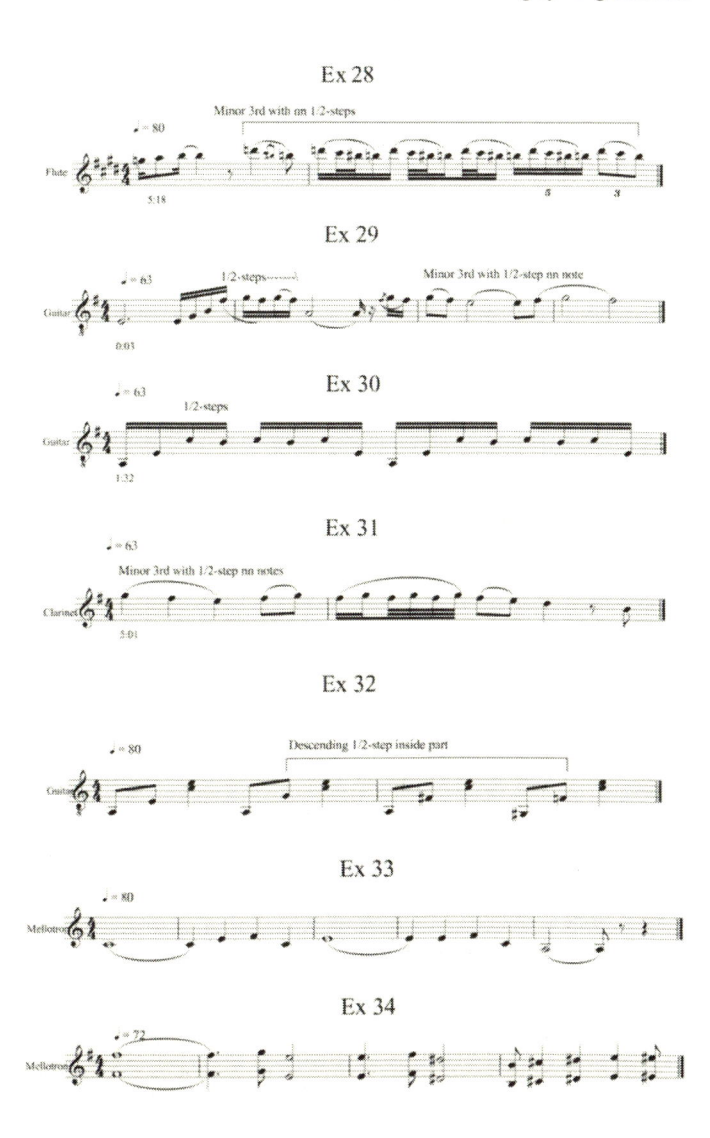

Musical Guide to In The Court Of The Crimson King by King Crimson

Ex 28

Ex 29

Ex 30

Ex 31

Ex 32

Ex 33

Ex 34

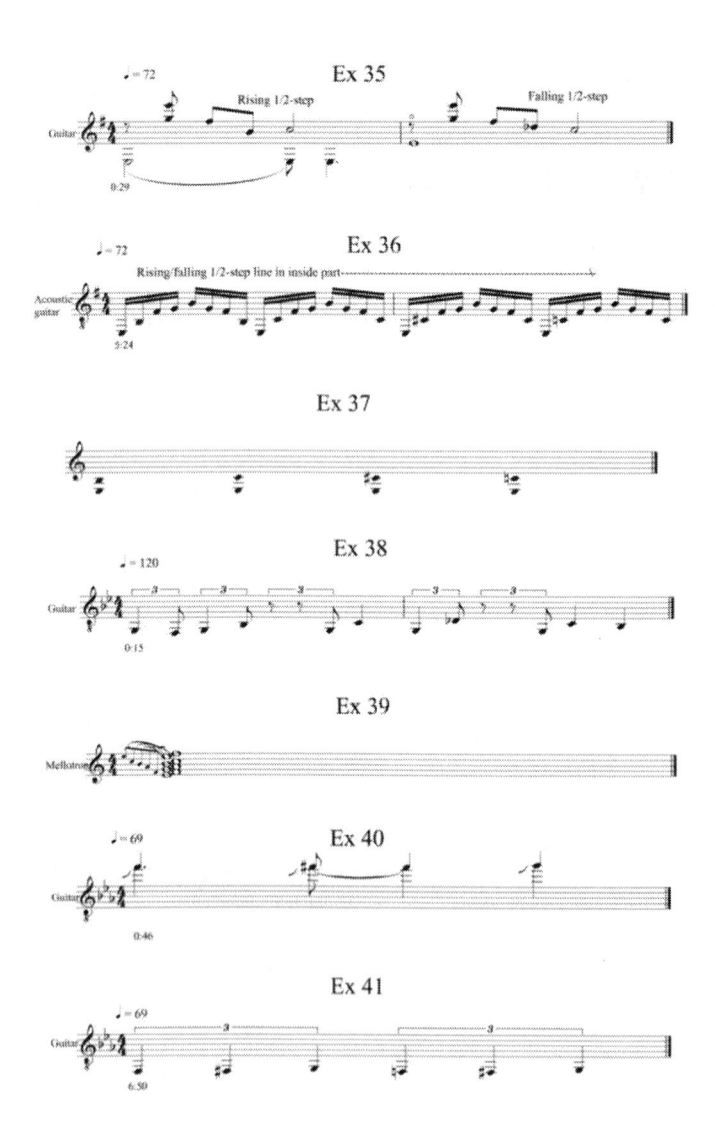

Musical Guide to In The Court Of The Crimson King by King Crimson

Ex 35

Ex 36

Ex 37

Ex 38

Ex 39

Ex 40

Ex 41

Musical Guide to In The Court Of The Crimson King by King Crimson

Ex 42

Ex 43

Ex 44

Ex 45

Ex 46

Ex 47

Ex 48

Musical Guide to In The Court Of The Crimson King by King Crimson

Musical Guide to In The Court Of The Crimson King by King Crimson

Ex 56

Ex 57

Ex 58

Ex 59

Ex 60

Ex 61

Musical Guide to In The Court Of The Crimson King by King Crimson

Ex. 62

Ex 63

Ex 64

Ex 65

Ex 66

Ex 67

Musical Guide to In The Court Of The Crimson King by King Crimson

Ex. 68

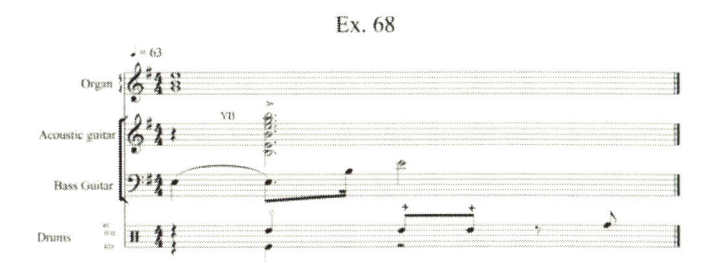

Ex. 69

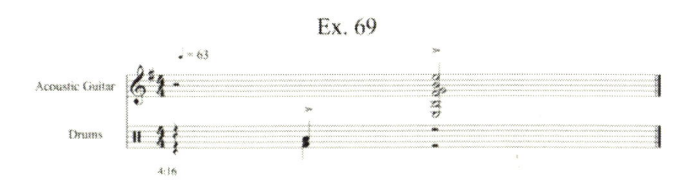

Ex 70

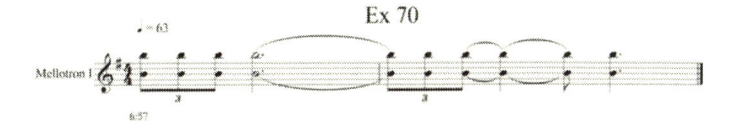

Ex. 71

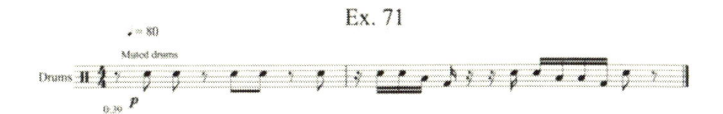

Ex 72

Musical Guide to In The Court Of The Crimson King by King Crimson

Diagram 1

	1. Schizoid Man	2. ITTTW	3. Epitaph	4. Moonchild	5. TCOTCK
Vox:	Treated	Natural	Natural	Treated (EQ)	Natural
WW/Reeds:	Sax (x2)	Flute/clarinet	Clari/bass clari.	—	Flute
Guitar:	Elec (dist.)	Guitar (clean)	Ac/electric	Electric	Ac/Electric
Bass:	x2 Clean/fuzz	Clean	Clean	—	Clean
Keys:	Pipe organ	Piano	Mel/ac.pno	Mel/vibes.	Mel/organ/hchord/pno
Drums:	Drums	Reduced drums	Timps/drums	Muted drums	Drums (Perc-like)

Musical Guide to In The Court Of The Crimson King by King Crimson

Diagram 2

Intro.	Ritornello	V.1	Ritorn.	V.2	Ritorn.	Rising ½ steps	Instrumental/Unison riffs	Ritorn.	V.3	Ritorn.	Coda
Organ	Band	Vox	Band	VoxA	Band	Band	Band	Band	Vox	Band	Band

Musical Guide to In The Court Of The Crimson King by King Crimson

Diagram 3

Ritornello	V.1	Chorus	V.2	Ch.	V.3	Ch.	Solo section (obbligato)	Solo (obbligato)	Ch.	V.1 Repeat	Ritorn.	Solo
Flutes	Vox	Full band	Vox	Full	Vox	Full	Flute	Guitar	Vox	Vox	Flutes	Flute

Musical Guide to In The Court Of The Crimson King by King Crimson

Diagram 4

Anacrusis	Ritornello	V.1	Ch.	Ritorn.	V.2	Anacrusis	Ritorn.	V.1 repeat	Chorus	Coda
Timpani	Guitar/mellotron	Vox	Vox	Gu/Mel	Vox	C dim.	Ac guita/claris	Vox	Vox	Full band + vox(s)

Musical Guide to In The Court Of The Crimson King by King Crimson

Diagram 5

Ritorn.	Chorus/Verse 1	Ritorn.	Chorus/Verse 2	Instrumental
Guitar-reverb signal	Vox	Guit.	Vox	Vibes, electric guitar and percussion.

Musical Guide to In The Court Of The Crimson King by King Crimson

Diagram 6

Ritorn.	V.1/Ch.	Ritorn.	V.2/Ch.	Ritorn.	Solo	Ritorn.	V.3/Ch.	Ritorn.	Solo	V.4/Ch. X3	Ritorn.	Rit. Variant	Ritorn. X6
Mel.	Vox	Mel.	Vox	Mel.	Mel.	Mel.	Vox	Mel.	Flute	Vox	Mel.	Pipe-organ	Mel +

Musical Guide to In The Court Of The Crimson King by King Crimson

Diagram 7

SM	ITTTW	Epitaph	Moonchild	TCOTCK
C minor	E major	E minor	A minor	E minor
Dorian	Mixolydian	Dorian	Aeolian	Aeolian
ACTIVE	PASSIVE	ACTIVE	PASSIVE	ACTIVE

Musical Guide to In The Court Of The Crimson King by King Crimson

Diagram 8

SM	ITTTW	Epitaph	Moonchild	TCOTCK
War/Counter-cultural reaction to Vietnam/Biafra/Nigeria situations.	Dialogue between straight man (employer) and a late man (young employee).	Counter-cultural hymn pointing-up folly of establishment (political/religious)	Vision of the (eternal)feminine epitomised by counter-culture.	Spin/greed of establishment powerbases.
(C minor/Dorian)	(E major/Mixolydian)	(E minor/Dorian)	(A minor/Aeolian)	(E minor/Aeolian)

Musical Guide to In The Court Of The Crimson King by King Crimson

Diagram 9

SM	ITTTW	Epitaph	Moonchild	TCOTCK
Negative	Positive	Negative	Positive	Negative
(C min.)	(E maj.)	(E min.)	(A min.)	(E min.)

Musical Guide to In The Court Of The Crimson King by King Crimson

Diagram 10

SM	ITTTW	Epitaph	Moonchild	TCOTCK
C minor		E minor		E minor

Major 3rd-related

E major

A Aeolian

5th-related

C

½-step-related

ends B major

12. The Sound World of In the Court of the Crimson King

Through the years there has been endless debate about aspects of King Crimson that differentiate them from other so-called Progressive rock bands and, in fact, it was they who became the musical model for the bands that followed. One of these has been their use of dynamics. Dynamic shaping is often part and parcel of the envelope occupied by orchestration and tension which, together with motif, harmony and phrasing, make a successful structure. I will discuss dynamics and will include these other aspects of the sound world of ITCOTCK. Although there were four playing members, King Crimson Mk I sometimes sounded orchestral, sometimes jazz-like. They also had a hard rock side, although no one style is exclusive to the band. It is this that presented the way forward for their contemporaries. I will also mention the studio side of things, and instrument settings used.

The hard-edged Schizoid Man is a perfect opener due to the impact it creates: raucous alto sax, played through a Marshall stack, doubled an octave lower by fuzz bass; the guitar supplying the chords and the second bass guitar anchoring the texture; drums are compressed. The bass and drums are brought into the foreground which was something of an innovation in 1969. The texture is reduced at the outset of verse one, with the treated vocal (distortion of the voice on the vocal channel) accompanied only by electric guitar and slightly-open hi-hat, four in a bar with equaliser altering the tone. Fripp says of his guitar sound: 'The sound: Les Paul guitar, bridge pick-up; Marshall stack with treble fully off, bass and middle fully cranked. I don't recall whether it was double-tracked, one high the other octave lower. The drive was cranked.' (96) The Mirrors section is in four parts: alto sax, guitar and bass powered by the drums, sax dropping out in the guitar solo and guitar dropping out in the double-tracked sax solo. Part of the mystery of ITCOTCK was as much to do with the fact that the instruments heard couldn't be identified with what had been familiar, in terms of their sound, in rock up to that point in time. For example, the double sax solo is so distorted that it is hardly recognisable as a sax. The solos very slightly lower the tension, except for the charging bass and drums. However, the saxes ascend to their high octave at the end of the solo (from 4:15ff.) winding-up the tension to breaking-point, preparing the recapitulation of the Mirrors riff. The 'stop-start' section, written by Fripp, is hammered-out at a slightly lower volume with a sudden lowering to *p* at 5:00 and a crescendo from 5:10ff. The climax in the coda with the volume taken to *fff*. It's possible to see the dynamic range and tension in connection with the structure: See Diagram 11 (at the end of this chapter).

Fripp says: 'Schizoid Man solo - played with a Burns Buzzaround fuzz box. The Burns unit didn't have enough volume for live, so that would have been a Foxy Lady or Fuzz Face, not used until I had a pedal-board built in 1970. Standard settings for metal area: treble pick-up, all bass and middle, no treble on Marshall/Hi-Watt top. The master volume was down, the pre-amp volume full up. Les Paul volume on 10. These would have changed with a fuzz box, but not sure what they might have been. Probably a relatively clean sound with solo sound tuned from the fuzz box.' (97)

The conjunct lines and rounded, soft timbre of I Talk to the Wind come as a complete contrast to the angularity of the hard-edged Schizoid Man. The orchestration - I am reluctant to use the word 'arrangement' in the context of the present discussion - is apt for the dialogue subject of the lyrics. For example, there are two flutes, two clarinets and two vocal parts. During the introduction and verse the timbre is enhanced by the soft piano accompaniment. The ascending flute line in the chorus is mostly in semibreves, as well as being a good example of Ian McDonald's orchestration skills, with a counter-melody concentrated on painting the words, 'I talk to the wind/My words are all carried away.' See Example 73. A soft, clean electric guitar responds to the flute on harmonics and glissandi in a descending line which, against the flute's rising line, creates tension towards the phrase ending: See Example 74. The piano accompaniment is there, but barely audible. This kind of orchestration is meaningful, serving the song and enlivening the lyrics. Verse two steps-up the clarinet duet. The pitches are played in the warm chalumeau register adding to the roundedness of the song: See Example 75. The clarinets in verse three elaborate those of verse two by adding passing-notes. The middle and end flute solos are examples of McDonald's improvisatory skills, with a guitar solo from 3:15ff effectively shaped to bring out the ½-steps. The drumming relies on delicate cymbals first heard in the introduction and first verse or the passage at the end of the chorus which illustrates Giles' jazz technique: See Example 76. The drums are shifted from left to right in the stereo-field from 4:47ff. The middle flute solo is underpinned by soft tom-toms, and long organ chords secure the harmony. The cross-fade at the end (6:02ff.) segues into Epitaph.

Epitaph is the powerful piece placed in the centre of the structure of ITCOTCK. It is introduced by a crescendo on timpani coming out of the fade of the previous ITTTW. It's as though ITTTW and Epitaph are like the Yin and Yang of one large piece. The portentous music is strengthened by the inclusion of KC's major musical weapon: the mellotron. Epitaph is symphonic but, compared to The Moody Blues or even The Beatles who also used the instrument, the sound here is overwhelming. Ian McDonald remembers, 'I used a Marshall double-stack for the mellotron and placed the microphone twenty-five feet away. There was inherent distortion when the volume was cranked-up.' (98) See Example 77.

The mellotron is reinforced by a crash-cymbal on the downbeat of the first and fifth bars, and from 0:15 cymbals and timpani create a massive crescendo into the downbeat of 0:19. The clean electric guitar's ½-step melodic motif is accompanied by acoustic guitar and underpinned by the bass guitar's ground. The music arrives at a pause at 0:35 bridged by the acoustic guitar's B Major arpeggio figurations. The first half of verse one is just voice, bass and drums (snare and kick-drum). The snare, played on beats two and four, are in the foreground giving the music the intense funereal quality. At the words 'Upon the instruments of death' the mellotron fades-in (0:56), and at 'when every man is torn apart' acoustic guitar attacks the E Minor9th chord sul ponticello, providing the music with expressive word-painting: See Example 78. There is a build-up in intensity towards the chorus. As the voice declaims 'Confusion will be my epitaph' the music is suspended, so to speak, the organ holding single four-beat chords. The organ's role here has a distant similarity to the sho in Japanese Gagaku ceremonial music: See Example 79, as well as The Beatles' We Can Work It Out.

Loud double-octave bass E's and B's are played by the piano at the beginning of each bar, reinforcing the bass guitar part: See Example 80. Acoustic guitar and drums play on the second beats of each bar: See Example 81.

The full band enter at 2:02 with mellotron crotchets building to 2:27. A repeat of the introduction, this time powered by drums playing 'drags' on beats three of each bar. Giles' drumming style was one of the key factors of King Crimson's success. It was a style to which drummers such as Carl Palmer, Guy Evans, Bill Bruford and Andy McCullough referred. His restraint, in the service of the music and as an integral part of the orchestration, is remarkable. Verse three is more flowing with Fripp's cross-picked guitar. The anacrusis from the introduction makes a re-appearance, this time as the huge upsurge on a C Diminished seventh chord, a typical nineteenth century modulatory technique. See Example 82.

After a massive accent on the downbeat at 3:57, a solo acoustic passage connects with the section for clarinet and bass clarinet playing in octaves in the section known as March for No Reason (4:16ff.). The profound darkness of this music owes much to the clarinets playing low octaves, the tom-tom attacks, the bass guitar on beat one and the guitar on beat three: See Example 83. Again the music is dark and slow-moving, with all the instruments in their low registers. The repeat of the first verse and chorus returns to the flowing accompaniment with acoustic guitar strumming chords rather than picking. This in turn leads to the repeated C Major - B Minor coda called Tomorrow and Tomorrow, memorable because of its non-resolution and sheer power. The double-tracked mellotron parts recall the Scherzo of Beethoven's Fifth Symphony and Holst's Mars from The Planets Suite. See Example 84. Mellotron I occasionally ascends to C, again emphasising the ½-step. In fact, it's just possible to hear the quotation from Mars occurring from time to time from 7:39ff in the purely instrumental section at the tail-end of the coda. Ian McDonald makes direct reference to the 5/4 ostinato of the Holst, which King Crimson were playing in their 'live' shows in 1969. This may well be the first reference in King Crimson's music to polymetres which became so important in the band's subsequent output. The timpani are also used to great effect with crescendos on beats three and four leading to massive accents on the downbeats of subsequent bars. Greg Lake's vocals are notable throughout the album, demonstrating the singularly expressive quality he brought to King Crimson. Dynamics tend to be brought about through the use of orchestral accumulations, coinciding with the harmony: See Diagram 12.

Moonchild is a song which seems to have some affinity with the early Renaissance consort song genre, originally a form using voice and viols. Its subject is the feminine, nodding in the direction of the Troubadours and the subject of Courtly Love. (I am grateful to Jacob Heringman for this insight). If this is the case, then the music of Moonchild, and TCOTCK (both originally included as the complete second side of the vinyl album) is appropriate. Certainly, the title-track refers to something ancient evoking a bygone time. The evocation of the ancient is also carried-over to Gini Barris' medieval-like illuminated manuscript sleeve, as well as to the lengthy, multi-sectional title-track of King Crimson's third album, Lizard. It might also be said that these ancient forms convey the message that spin and greed is an ever-present phenomenon. Moonchild is in four parts accompanying the vocal, with muted drums entering during the verse. The high guitar (the sound of the reverb signal) has the sound of a high mandolin or treble viol, which twice plays the vocal E-A-E motif, positioned left and then right in the stereo. Vibes accompany the downward motion of the rhythm guitar's ground (see Ex. 32) rounding-out the sound of the latter: See Example 85.

The mellotron plays a single line counter-melody (see Ex. 33). The vocal is soft, yet direct and close-up. Ian McDonald: 'I just had Greg sing very close to the microphone, and then put some EQ on it. The vocal is not in the centre of the stereo, but over to the right.' (99). I have discussed the three-part texture of the improvisation, but suffice to say it is both contemporary (jazz) and ancient at the same time; sustaining the atmosphere of the song in a haze of timeless resonance, appropriate for the evocation of the subtitles The Dream and The Illusion. Here the listener is transported into the visionary realm. Tension is at a minimum. In terms of dynamics, everything is held in abeyance, fitting for ancient musical forms where dynamics were yet to be codified.

TCOTCK is, essentially, a simple ballad (or ballade), and the consort-like orchestration is perfectly appropriate. In keeping with Moonchild, which precedes it, TCOTCK sounds ancient and folksong-like and yet contemporary at the same time. The dramatic ritornelli both introduce the verses and pause before each verse like an in-breath, with the sung verses the out-breath. The ritornello is for the full band and harmony vocals (choral-like) symbolising the softly singing choir in the lyrics of verse one. The verse is much reduced with instruments used in simple accompaniment roles. In verse one the guitar functions in a lute-like way, with flute as obbligato painting the words, 'The purple piper plays his tune.' Verse two includes imaginative use of drums in a death-march rhythm and the electric harpsichord flourish at the words, 'The cracked brass bells will ring'. (1:45) The section The Return of the Fire Witch symbolises flight with semi-quaver cymbals (2:20) accompanying a melodic mellotron line with oscillating bass guitar. Like all good orchestration it is simple and effective, never going beyond the main ideas with no extraneous music involved. Following the flute solo's semi-quaver sextuplets at 5:10, influenced by Rimsky-Korsakov's Scheherazade, a mellotron accumulation at 5:23 leads directly into verse four. The 'pulling of the strings' in the verse is painted by the bent electric guitar strings (5:49), and the chamber pipe-organ of Dance of the Puppets (7:17) provides a moment of respite before the sonic assault of the final ritornello.

Musical Guide to In The Court Of The Crimson King by King Crimson

Ex 73

Ex 74

Ex 75

Ex. 76

Ex 77

Ex 78

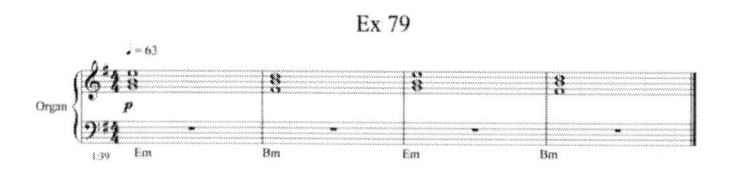

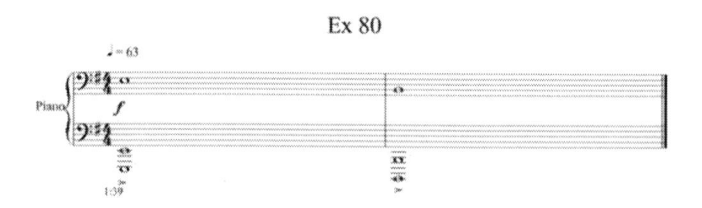

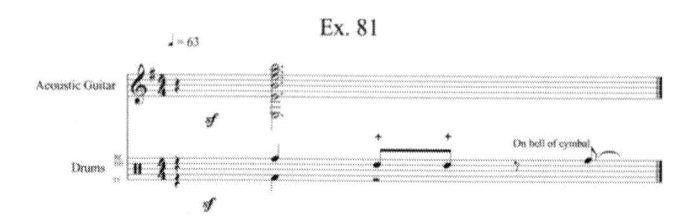

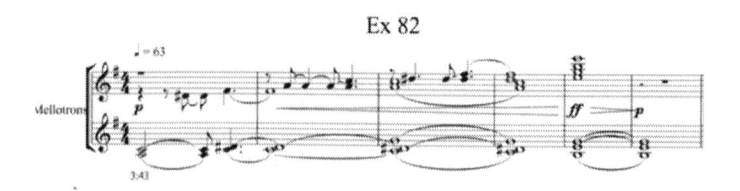

Musical Guide to In The Court Of The Crimson King by King Crimson

Ex 79

Ex 80

Ex. 81

Ex 82

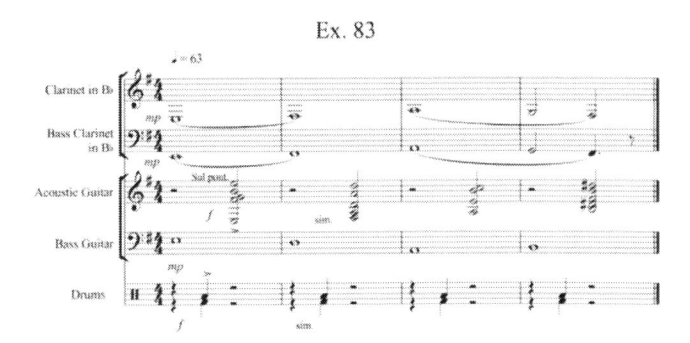

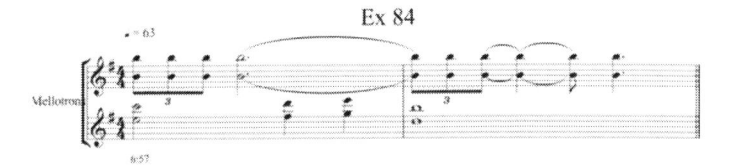

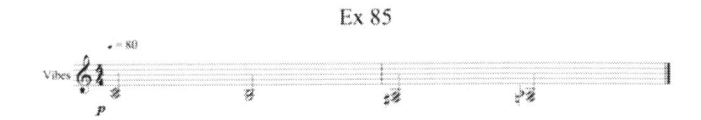

Musical Guide to In The Court Of The Crimson King by King Crimson

Ex. 83

Ex 84

Ex 85

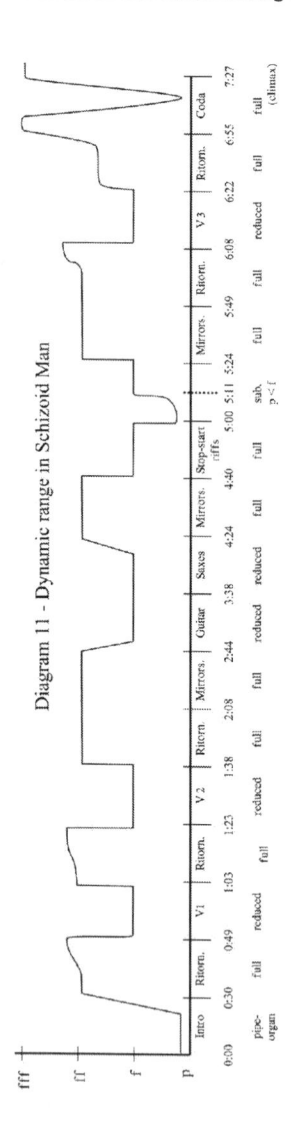

Musical Guide to In The Court Of The Crimson King by King Crimson

Diagram 11 - Dynamic range in Schizoid Man

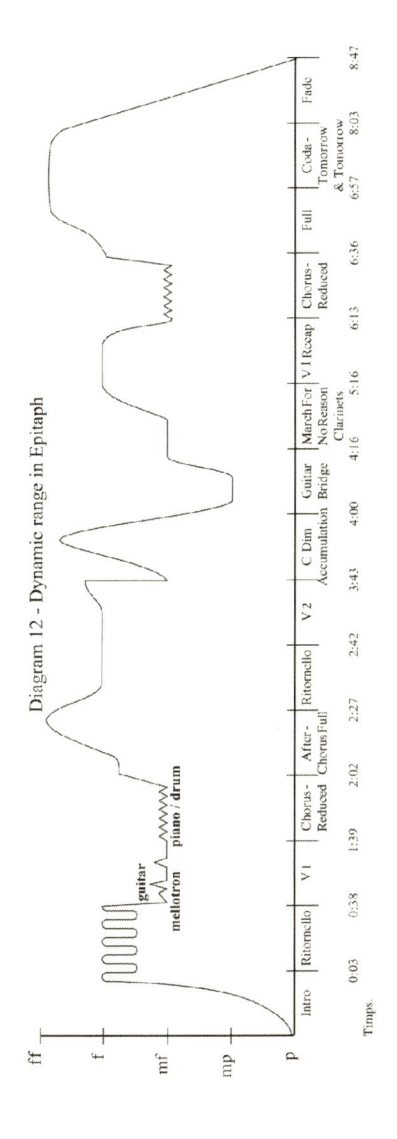

Musical Guide to In The Court Of The Crimson King by King Crimson

Diagram 12 - Dynamic range in Epitaph

13. Coda - Contextualising In the Court of the Crimson King

This discussion has been an attempt to contextualise ITCOTCK both from historical and analytical perspectives, alongside perspectives from the players themselves. Of course, there are compositional techniques, some consciously applied and some not; musical influences and the input of the players; the *zeitgeist*.

Looking at the music of this and subsequent King Crimson albums, it's clear that a common musical thread winds its way through the band's recorded output. Robert Fripp has talked about the 'spirit of King Crimson' which isn't an element necessarily visible in the outputs of the various members' . The one common element to King Crimson is Fripp himself, and Miles Davis and jazz has provided a model for the various Crimson incarnations. 'Miles (Davis) was an influence, not quite directly and not quite musically. More, an influence in approach to being a player. The bands that were models were not rock groups but jazz outfits; and the players, the jazz players. Miles bands: a strong pattern validating the different models of King Crimson. Tony Williams (Live in Japan!!!) astonishing. This was more a direct musical influence. Lifetime were breathtaking. I stopped listening closely because it would have distracted me.'

(100) Fripp has employed and played alongside other musicians to complete the various ingredients important to King Crimson, unavailable to himself personally. For example, by grounding the poetic, pure rock and classical sides of the various members that have passed through the ranks of King Crimson through his own approach to musical technique and intense practical discipline, Fripp has been able to forge a multi-faceted band. This process was probably unconscious for Fripp himself at the time of ITCOTCK, becoming apparent with each subsequent incarnation. Certainly, he regarded Adrian Belew (King Crimson's other guitar player from 1981 onwards) as his 'other' side - the side unavailable to him - in terms of guitar techniques.

After ITCOTCK nothing was ever quite the same again for art-rock. King Crimson set the playing, recording and writing standards for the subsequent Progressive rock bands. For example, Van der Graaf Generator's Pawn Hearts, Genesis' Foxtrot, Yes' Time and a Word and Renaissance's eponymous album (which also has five song-pieces) were all influenced by ITCOTCK. Even Deep Purple (the riff from Into the Fire, from Deep Purple in Rock, is a transformation of the Schizoid Man ritornello riff) and Black Sabbath (Paranoid) show the influence of King Crimson. Fripp: 'We were all young men on the scene at the time and knew each other's work. You probably are aware of King Crimson '69's influence on Yes. They were not as developed as King Crimson in 1969: they were still growing, but King Crimson landed fully grown. Bill (Bruford) told me that there were debates in Yes about the degree to which they would accept King Crimson influence. In 1970, Bill and Chris (Squire) did invite me to join, whether the rest of the band were aware of that or not. I played Catfood and Groon to Chris and Bill at my flat off the Portobello Road, and it clearly ignited them (particularly Bill). In 1971 Yes had the juice that King Crimson had in 1969. When the juice lands, it lands for a limited period of time and we are invited to take it and use it - invest it, blow it, coast on it.' (101) Fripp also says, 'My own view of ITCOTCK was that something else was going on. What, who knows? Looking back, I can see that the form of the album was important to the young Fripp. As I would now put it, a threshold was necessary to cross the liminal space between the outside and the inside.' (102)

In December 1969 the New Musical Express ran the headlines that Ian McDonald and Michael Giles had left the band. Early on in 1970, the music press brought the news that King Crimson would continue with Robert Fripp and Peter Sinfield at the helm, and later that year saw the release of In the Wake of Poseidon as well as the album from McDonald and Giles. Emerson, Lake and Palmer's first album was also released to great acclaim in November 1970. However, without ITCOTCK it's unlikely that these subsequent albums would ever have seen the light of day. In any style ITCOTCK is a high-point in British music. The playing, recording, songs, lyrics and sleeve-design convey a craft unparalleled in rock's history which combine to present a countercultural meta-narrative. In the Postmodern world this has, of course, been one of the criticisms of Progressive rock, regarded by some as the music of a white male elite. Greg Lake's view sums it up when he says 'King Crimson were a phenomenon.' Each of the players has gone on to forge equally unique paths: Fripp has continued King Crimson since that time, has featured as a solo musician (Frippertronics and Soundscapes), as a collaborator (Fripp and Eno etc.), as a session musician (David Bowie, Talking Heads, Blondie etc), producer (Peter Gabriel, Matching Mole etc.), teacher (Guitar Craft) and head of a record company (Discipline Global Mobile); Peter Sinfield has been a solo artist (Still), lyricist (Five Star, Bucks Fizz), collaborator (ELP, Greg Lake), writer, poet and lecturer (BMI) and producer (Roxy Music, PFM); Greg Lake has been a member of Emerson, Lake and Palmer, a producer (Spontaneous Combustion), soloist and collaborator (with Peter Sinfield); Michael Giles has been a much sought-after session player, collaborator (McDonald and Giles, Giles, Muir and Cunningham), soloist (the album, Progress) and band member (21st Century Schizoid Band, the Mad Band); Ian McDonald has been a soloist (Drivers Eyes), writer- collaborator (McDonald and Giles), co-founder of Foreigner, producer (Daryl Way's Wolf etc.), session musician (T.Rex etc.) and member of the 21st Century Schizoid Band. The concepts of ITCOTCK - without ever subscribing to the term 'concept album' - will be relevant to future generations because, ultimately, it is an observation of the human condition. Not only is ITCOTCK a protest, it is a satire: pointing-up both the folly and the illusory nature of establishment thinking as well as the plasticity of the period, it is not only a reactionary DIY objet d'art but, at the same time, a fantasy through its use of polystylism which includes references to jazz, rock, folk and art and film music. Like the subject of the 1960's TV series The Prisoner and the later movie The Truman Show, it demonstrates establishment manipulation of the individual by political and religious means.

Finally, I asked Robert Fripp just how the writing process worked in King Crimson Mk I as, through the years, I've sensed the high degree of musical unity within it. I will leave the final word to him: 'It was a "band mind". King Crimson had a wholeness about it, until around July 1969, mainly because of a unity of aim and commitment. Early success and the personal matters of young men dispersed the focus. But enough was moving to carry us towards the end of the year. It was a tragedy that the band broke up, whatever the inevitability. My own view of the process at work is probably rather different from the other members. The Good Fairy was a creative power at work that acted upon and through the young men; it did not originate in them. The contributions of all of them was necessary, and no one person can be credited with providing the Fairy Dust!' (103)

Bibliographical Notes

1) Allan F. Moore - Rock: The Primary Text (Ashgate, 2001) p. 109ff.
2) Sid Smith - In the Court of King Crimson (Helter Skelter, 2001)
3) Ibid. p. 15ff.
4) All the dates are taken from Robert Fripp's Journal included in The Young Person's Guide to King Crimson (EG Music Ltd. 1974).
5) CD: King Crimson - Live in Hyde Park, July 5th, 1969. The King Crimson Collector's Club, Club 12. DGM, 2002.
6) Robert Fripp Journal. Op. cited.
7) Iain Cameron - Email to the author, 4-03-03.
8) Sid Smith - Op. cited, p.26.
9) Michael Giles - telephone conversation with the author, Feb. 2003.
10) Robert Fripp - Email to the author, 27-03-03.
11) Sid Smith - Op. cited, p.38.
12) Robert Fripp - sleeve-notes from booklet.
13) Iain Cameron - Email to the author, March 2003.
14) Lecture given by Peter Sinfield at the BMI, London, 1997.
15) Peter Sinfield - Email to the author, 2001.
16) Peter Sinfield - telephone conversation with the author, 9-03-03.
17) Peter Sinfield - Email to the author, 11-07-02.
18) Robert Fripp - Email to the author, 27-03-03.
19) Andrew Keeling - Musical Guide to Larks' Tongues in Aspic - www.larkstonguesinaspic.ukf.net
20) Email to the author, July 2001.
21) Ibid.

22) Robert Fripp - Email to the author, 27-03-03.
23) Ian McDonald - Email to the author, 8-03-01.
24) Ian McDonald - telephone conversation with the author, 6-04-03
25) Email, 26-06-01.
26) Telephone conversation, 6-03-01.
27) Peter Sinfield - Email to the author, 15-03-03.
28) Peter Sinfield - Email to the author, 17-07-02.
29) Peter Sinfield . BMI Lecture, London, 1997.
30) Peter Sinfield - Email to the author, 15-03-03.
31) Peter Sinfield - Email to the author, 26-06-01.
32) Peter Sinfield - Email to the author, 15-03-03.
33) Peter Sinfield - Email to the author, 6-01-03.
34) Peter Sinfield - Email to the author, 23-12-01.
35) Michael Giles - telephone conversation with the author, 7-04-03.
36) Ian McDonald - telephone conversation with the author, February, 2003.
37) Ibid.
38) Robert Fripp - Email to the author, 28-03-03.
39) C.G. Jung - The Phenomenology of the Spirit in Fairytales in Archetypes of the Collective Unconscious. Collected Works, Vol. 9, Pt. 1. (RKP, London, 1959). P. 208ff.
40) Ibid. p.211.
41) Ibid. p.212.
42) Conversation with Michael Giles, 7-04-03.
43) C.G. Jung - Collected Works Vol. 9, Pt. 1. P.211.
44) John Ruskin - Sesame and Lilies, the Two Paths. (Everyman Library, 1907). P. 109-110.
45) Cedric Watts - A Preface to Keats. (Longman Group, 1985). P. 65-67.
46) Peter Sinfield - Email to the author, 17-07-02.
47) Ibid.
48) Stuart Nicholson - Jazz Rock. (Canongate Books). P. 7ff.
49) Quotation by Robert Fripp. Unknown source.
50) Sid Smith - Op. cited. p.49.
51) Robert Fripp - Journal. Op. cited.
52) Ibid. Aug. 29th, 1969.
53) Email to the author, 13-04-03.
54) Ibid.
55) Edward Macan - Rocking the Classics - English Progressive Rock and the Counterculture. (Oxford, 1997). p. 11. By permission of Oxford University Press Inc. www.oup.com
56) Ibid.
57) Archie Loss - Pop Dreams - Music, Movies and the Media in the 1960's. (Harcourt Brace and Co. 1999). p. 117.
58) Ibid. p.29.
59) Edward Macan - Op. cited. p.21.
60) Ibid. p.29.
61) Ibid. p.23.

62) Ibid. p.41. and Keeling - Op. cited.
63) Ibid. p.50.
64) Ian McDonald - telephone conversation with the author, 16-02-03.
65) Allan F. Moore - Op. cited. p.111ff.
66) Ibid. p.112.
67) Ibid.
68) Ibid. p.113.
69) Peter Sinfield - Email to the author, 13-04-2003.
70) Booklet from King Crimson, Epitaph. DGM 9607. P.16.
71) Peter Sinfield - Telephone conversation with the author, 6-03-03.
72) Ian McDonald - Telephone conversation with the author, 7-04-03.
73) Peter Sinfield - Telephone conversation with the author, 6-03-03.
74) Peter Sinfield and Jon Green. Promenade the Puzzle. www.songsouponsea.com
75) Peter Sinfield Lecture at the BMI.
76) Sid Smith - Op. cited77) Ibid. p.70.
78) Ibid.
79) Ian McDonald - telephone conversation with the author, 6-04-06.
80) Ibid.
81) Stephanie Ruben - telephone conversation with the author, 2001.
82) Robert Fripp - Email to the author, 5-04-05.
83) Peter Sinfield - telephone conversation with the author, Spring 2002.
84) Ian McDonald - telephone conversation with the author, 6-04-05.
85) Ibid, 18-05-04.
86) Ibid.
87) Ibid.
88) Ian McDonald - telephone conversation with the author, 6-04-03.
89) Robert Fripp - email to the author, 5-04-05.
90) Ian McDonald - telephone conversation with the author, 6-04-03.
91) Peter Sinfield - telephone conversation with the author, 9-01-09.
92) Sid Smith - In the Court of King Crimson (Helter Skelter, 2001. p.67).
93) Robert Fripp - email to the author, 10-01-09.
94) Ian McDonald - email to the author, 20-01-09.
95) Robert Fripp - email to the author, 19-01-09.
96) Robert Fripp - email to the author, 26-05-04.
97) Robert Fripp - email to the author, 26-10-04.
98) Ian McDonald - telephone conversation with the author, 6-04-03.
99) Ian McDonald - email to the author, 14-01-09.
100) Robert Fripp - email to the author, 21-06-06.
101) Robert Fripp - email to the author, 9-03-06.
102) Robert Fripp - email to the author, 10-01-09.
103) Robert Fripp - Ibid.

Bibliography

(All bibliographical material has been used by permission although one or two sources couldn't be contacted or didn't respond to repeated attempts to make contact. For this we apologise.)

Robert Fripp - Journal to The Young Person's Guide to King Crimson - EG Music Ltd., 1974.

C.G. Jung - Archetypes of the Collected Unconscious, Vol. 9, Pt. 1 - RKP, London, 1959.

Archie Loss - Pop Dreams, Music, Movies and the Media in the 1960's - Harcourt Brace & Co, 1999.

Edward Macan - Rocking the Classics - English Progressive Rock and the Counterculture. - Oxford OUP, 1997.

Allan F. Moore - Rock: The Primary Text - Ashgate, 2001.

Stuart Nicholson - Jazz Rock - Canongate Books, 1998.

Peter Sinfield - Lecture at the BMI, London, 1977

Sid Smith - In the Court of King Crimson - Helter Skelter, 2001.

Links

Andrew Keeling - www.andrewkeeling.ukf.net

David Cross and Noisy Records - www.david-cross.com

Greg Lake - www.greglake.com

Mark Graham (Spaceward) - www.markgraham.ukf.net

Michael Giles - www.michaelgiles.com

Peter Sinfield - www.songsouponsea.com

Robert Fripp, King Crimson and DGM Live - www.dgmlive.com

Sid Smith - http://sidsmith.blogspot.com

Musical Guide to In The Court Of The Crimson King by King Crimson

Photographs

Photographs by courtesy of DGM Art Department - with special thanks to Hugh O'Donnel.

Musical Guide to In The Court Of The Crimson King by King Crimson

Michael Giles and Peter Sinfield

Musical Guide to In The Court Of The Crimson King by King Crimson

Greg Lake and Robert Fripp

Ian McDonald

Musical Guide to In The Court Of The Crimson King by King Crimson

Michael Giles

Musical Guide to In The Court Of The Crimson King by King Crimson

Ian McDonald at the Marquee Club

Musical Guide to In The Court Of The Crimson King by King Crimson

Greg Lake at the Marquee Club

Musical Guide to In The Court Of The Crimson King by King Crimson

Michael Giles, Robert Fripp and Ian McDonald backstage at the Marquee Club

Robert Fripp at the Marquee Club

Musical Guide to In The Court Of The Crimson King by King Crimson

Peter Sinfield

Musical Guide to In The Court Of The Crimson King by King Crimson

Robert Fripp at Hyde Park

About The Author

Andrew Keeling's association with King Crimson goes back to 1969 when he first heard In the Court of the Crimson King. He is a composer and musician living in the North of England and has a PhD from the University of Manchester. His orchestrations of Robert Fripp's Soundscapes were performed by the Metropole Orchestra in Amsterdam in 2003 and, as a flautist, he has recently formed an improvisation duo with former King Crimson violinist David Cross.

Coming soon from Spaceward...

Also by Andrew Keeling

**Musical Guide to Larks' Tongues In Aspic
by King Crimson**

and

**Musical Guide to In The Wake Of Poseidon
by King Crimson**

First published in CD-ROM format and now extensively revised
and made available in book form for the first time.

blurb.com